Good Morning
Uncle Sam

Andrew Miles

"I pledge allegiance to the flag of the United States of America, and to the republic for which it stands, one nation under God, indivisible, with liberty and justice for all."

This book is dedicated to Zephaniah "Doc" and Eunabelle Miles and all of their descendants. The blood of Mississippi sharecroppers runs through each of us and is the source of our decency, strength, determination, and tenacity. It bonds the generations despite the distances that separate us. Our grandparents produced two of the greatest men I've ever known—my father, Charles Miles, and his brother Johnny. In their own way, each taught us what it means to be a man—to love unconditionally, to live respectfully, and to value family.

I am eternally indebted to Palmer Home for Children in Columbus, Mississippi. They have provided a home for so many children and helped to produce the most elegant and graceful of women— my mother. She has been a source of strength and a remarkable example of resilience.

April, thank you for your patience and words of encouragement. Just as my mother inspired my father, you have inspired me. I will forever love you!

To my beautiful daughters, Jennifer and Michelle — I am so very proud of you both, and love you both so much!

I want to especially thank all the American men and women who—despite the difficulty, manage to make it on their own.

Yes, I served in the army
It's where I learned to shoot
Eighteen months in the desert
Pourin' sand out of my boots

No, I've never been convicted of a crime
I could start this job at any time.

I got a strong back, Steel toes
I rarely call in sick, a good truck
What I don't know, I catch on real quick
I work weekends, If I have to Nights and holidays
Give you 40 And then some
Whatever it takes

Ronnie Dunn "Cost of Livin"

Contents

ANDREW MILES—*GOOD MORNING, UNCLE SAM*

Chapter 1

Good Morning, Uncle Sam

It's early morning at the Old Soldiers Home, a retirement facility for America's aging and oft forgotten veterans.

A police officer walks into a room and leans over the bed of a man who had once been America's greatest hero.

"Good morning Uncle Sam, it's time to wake up. Come on old man, I know that you don't want to, but you must open your eyes.

In an almost child-like manner, Uncle Sam rubs his eyes and says, "Please, just a few more years."

Irritated and already tired from working an over night shift at a second job, the police officer shakes Uncle Sam and tells him, "No, we're running out of time, you must wake up and face the world. You've

United we stand, divided we fall.

been asleep for so long, and you have a lot of catching up to do."

Grumpily, Uncle Sam slowly lifts himself from the bed and crosses the room to stretch in front of his favorite window. "Why are these bars on the window and why can I no longer see Lady Liberty from here?"

With shame in his voice, the police officer breaks the bad news to Uncle Sam. "While you were sleeping, we lost control of the nation, and the bars are there because people keep trying to break in to steal what little you have left. But that's not what's blocking your view of Lady Liberty— she's no longer there. The special interests groups finally got the best of her and she had to be committed."

"What? How long have I been asleep?"

"I guess that it has been decades, and things have really changed. It's not the hard working and decent America that you once knew."

Walking to the closet, the officer takes out a set of clothes and a top hat, and hands them to Uncle Sam. "Get dressed, you can ride with me today and see how things really are."

"If it is as bad as you say, I will need a gun."

"You probably do need one, but American's no longer have the right to bear arms without a permit, and you don't have one. Put this vest on though. If you get shot it might stop the bullet."

God Bless America!

They leave Uncle Sam's room and walk down the long hallway to the lobby, where several elderly veterans are gathered around the television watching Fox News. The lead story concerns the debt crisis and congress' failure to act on it. The men spot Uncle Sam, and they all rise as he approaches. "Uncle Sam" yells an old man, with but one leg. "You've got to go back to Washington and fix this unbelievable mess that we are in."

"Boys, I'm tired and bloodied, and don't know that I have the strength."

Putting his arm around Uncle Sam's shoulders, the police officer offers encouragement. "You can do it Uncle Sam, and we'll all do our part as well. But first, let's hit the streets so that you can see first-hand how things really are."

As soon as they are in the police car and have checked in-service, they are sent to a shooting.

"This is in the projects, so watch your back. I'd hate for you to get hurt."

"What kind of project are they working on that someone would get shot?"

Chuckling, the officer informs Uncle Sam that it is not a construction project. "They're housing projects, places where people can live for free."

"Why then, if they live for free, are they so unhappy that they are shooting each other?"

United we stand, divided we fall.

Knowingly, the officer replies, "Drugs and welfare, Uncle Sam. They've all but destroyed our nation."

Arriving at the scene of the shooting, Uncle Sam is shocked to see row upon row of buildings and he is alarmed by the number of people loitering about. "Lord, the sun has been up for two hours already. These people better hurry or they'll be late for work."

Laughing so hard that he must spit his coffee out, the officer reminds Uncle Sam that not everyone must work. "Remember, they live for free."

Puzzled, Uncle Sam can only say, "That just doesn't seem right!"

"I guess that depends on which way you lean Uncle Sam. To the left or to the right."

Lifting the crime scene tape, the officer and Uncle Sam walk towards the body of yet another dead young man. "See that baggie next to the body? That, Uncle Sam, is crack cocaine and it has caused so many problems."

With saddened eyes, Uncle Sam surveys the crowd and then suddenly grabs the officer by the arm. Angrily, he says, "Tell that young girl to get her baby sister away from here. They are both too young to see something as horrible as this."

"That's not her sister Uncle Sam, that's her daughter."

"Oh, dear God."

God Bless America!

Several hours later, this portion of the investigation is complete, and all of the officers go back in service. As they are leaving the housing projects, a call comes across the radio – upon returning from work, an elderly victim found that his home had been burglarized. The officer advises that they will take it.

As they are driving, the officer quizzes Uncle Sam's memory. "Do you remember how, after the Great War, you guaranteed loans for returning veterans to buy homes?"

"Of course I do. Our veterans have sacrificed so much for our freedoms."

"Well, these are the neighborhoods they built when they returned."

Looking around, Uncle Sam sees only run-down houses, overgrown yards, and people everywhere. "How in the world did this happen? Did we lose a war?"

"No, just our pride and our common sense. These are mostly Section 8 houses and, like the projects, the tenants do not have to pay rent, so they take no pride in their homes."

Puzzled, Uncle Sam scratches his beard and ponders the obvious. "Well, someone has to pay for all of this, so please, say it's not me."

"At one time, you did pay for it all. But now that you are broke, we have to borrow the money needed from China or other countries."

United we stand, divided we fall.

"Broke? I once had enough money that we were the envy of all nations."

"Yeah, well, taking care of so many non-working people has really piled on the debt. You owe $15 trillion, and tack on billions more each day."

Uncle Sam silently stares out the passenger window for the remainder of the ride until suddenly, he spots the Stars and Stripes waving proudly from a flagpole in the front yard of a well-maintained home. "Look at that Andrew, isn't she beautiful. There's just something about seeing Old Glory that makes everything seem better."

"Yeah, she is, and that happens to be the home that we are going to."

As they park, an elderly and hunched over man slowly makes his way down the drive. When he sees Uncle Sam his shoulders instinctively straighten, his chin braces, and for a moment, he resembles the twenty year old Marine that he'd once been. "Uncle Sam, where have you been? We've needed you so badly! Did you forget about us?"

"No Joe, I could never forget about you; you were a hero at Guadalcanal, and took one to the chest on Iwo Jima. You're a part of the greatest generation this nation has ever known, and I owe you so much!" With his head down, and as he wipes away a tear, Uncle Sam tells Joe how sorry he is that he must live like this.

God Bless America!

Taken aback by Uncle Sam's show of emotion, Joe attempts to make him feel better—"It's okay Uncle Sam, they only stole my television and I can replace it, just as I've had to do several times before."

Uncle Sam reaches out to Joe and places a hand on his shoulder. "You shouldn't have to live like this. Why are you still here?"

Joe turns his head towards his house, and a smile comes across his face as he reflects on the last sixty years. "Jane and I built this home after the war and we raised our children here. God, I miss her so much! These thugs can steal my property, but I'll be damned if I let them force me to abandon my memories. I could never move. I did not back down in battle, and I will not now back down to the crips, bloods, or whatever else they want to call themselves. This is my home. The problem is that they wait until I leave for work to break in; otherwise, I'd show them the business end of a Marine issued, Ka-Bar knife."

Not doubting Joe's tenacity, Uncle Sam is no less concerned for his safety. "Like me Joe, you're getting old. Why don't you just retire, and stay home?"

"I did, but without a cost of living increase to my Social Security, and the higher costs of Medicare, I just couldn't make ends meet. So now I greet everyone as they enter WalMart. It's not a bad job, but standing for so long sure makes my back hurt."

United we stand, divided we fall.

Though the conversation with Joe was a nice respite, the police officer had to finish gathering the information needed for the report. When that was done, it was time to get back on the streets— calls were stacking up. "Sir, looks like we have everything we need. Is there anything else that we can do for you?"

"Short of parking your car in my driveway officer, I guess not."

"Well sir, thank you for your service, and I will try to get some extra police patrols through your neighborhood. I really wish that I could do more! I hope that your day gets better."

"It will officer, after all, it's America!"

As they get back into their patrol car, both sit silently for a moment and watch as the old man nails a sheet of plywood to the frame of his broken out window. "Come on Uncle Sam, let's get you home. You're looking tired and really haggard. You need to get some rest."

"Have you lost your mind?" Uncle Sam says to the officer. "There is no time for rest. We've made a complete mess of things and destroyed all that we once had. Somehow, we must fix this. Let's get everyone together so that we can discuss our battle plan."

God Bless America!

"Are you kidding, Uncle Sam? There's no getting everyone together. There's too much distance between the left and the right, and those in the middle work too much and don't seem to have the time."

"We're not just going to give up; the sleeping giant has awakened, and we will rally the troops! We are not just Democrats, Republicans, or Tea Partiers. We're Americans first and foremost! Let's talk about this over dinner, my treat. But first, stop at that ATM so that I can get some money out. After all that I have seen and heard today, I can only hope that there's at least a little left."

Yet again confused, Uncle Sam looks to the officer for assistance. "Why is this asking me to press one for English?"

"That's a whole 'nother story, Uncle Sam."

United we stand, divided we fall.

Chapter 2

Good Morning, America

Good morning, America, it's Uncle Sam, and it's time to wake the hell up! Pull the blanket down from your eyes; it won't shield you from the problems that our nation faces! I've let you down, and I am sorry for that, but I am back and with a vengeance.

I have ridden with my nephew and his brothers in blue and have seen firsthand the problems that we face. We can fix them, but not from inside your glass houses; the view is too pretty from there. We have to get into the trenches, smell the blood, see the guts, and hear the screams. Then we will understand!

We must put away our special interests and focus on the problems that can destroy us now, not in 10,000 years. Gay rights, abortion, gun rights, the whales, global warming, and everything else are all

United we stand, divided we fall.

important topics and deserve their time in the spotlight—just not right now!

It is time for our politicians—the ones whom *we* elected, to put aside their childish ways and start behaving like the adults they are. They must control themselves for just a little longer and focus on the job at hand.

Stop having affairs, photographing your "Weiners" and embarrassing yourselves and us in other ways. For just a few months, put the nation before General Electric, General Motors, and all other corporate giants. I realize they fund your coffers, but this is more important.

Put aside your partisan ways, and come back to the middle for just a while. Let's all shake hands and behave like ladies and gentlemen so that we can intelligently discuss our issues rather than point fingers and place blame.

We all caused this, each and every one of us. Presidents Bush and Obama are no more to blame for our problems than President George Washington. The problems have been generations in the making, and we have had ample opportunity to address them. Instead, we only bickered.

Individual rights and civil liberties are important; they are the foundation upon which our country is built. However, just because people feel they

God Bless America!

are entitled to something doesn't mean that they should get it.

It is within your rights to stand in front of the White House and say whatever you want; it is purely a symbol of government. You should not, however, have the right to disrupt the funeral of a fallen soldier because you think God hates homosexuals. I cannot believe that we have such people in this nation!

What happened to our polite society? Was it political correctness that led to decency and respect being vanquished into the history books only to become faded memories? Or did it happen when we took God out of everything because nonbelievers were offended?

God does belong in our schools and in every other aspect of our lives. After all, we are "one nation, under God," and it is "in God we trust."

It was written that "Congress shall make no law respecting an establishment of religion," but what our founders meant was that Congress could not declare that we all had to be of one belief. They never intended that government be void of God. In fact, they appealed to the "Supreme Judge of the world" for their moral rightness in the signing of the Declaration of Independence.

Speaking of independence…it is our national treasure—an idea that many have defended with

United we stand, divided we fall.

their lives—and I wonder how we have allowed so many of our citizens to lose theirs? We take money from those who work and through entitlements we give it to the laziest among us, who then, become dependent upon our support.

We have become so concerned about the rights of a select few that we have made life more difficult for many. Our focus should be on crime, education, illegal immigration, and the abuse of public entitlements. We can address everything else once we have stopped the bleeding.

Wake up, America; Uncle Sam needs *you!*

Chapter 3

The American Middle

Fueled by overall unhappiness with the state of the nation, waves of distrust and unrest are rolling across America unlike anything experienced since the Boston Tea Party of 1773.

Frustrations are rising, and more people today (43 percent) than ever before feel that the government has a negative impact on their lives.

From the working class to the upper middle class, the topics of conversation are the same, varying only by degree. Whether speaking with a doctor or an assembly line worker, one gets the sense of an overall disgust with the direction the nation has taken in matters of:

- the economy
- health care
- crime and punishment

United we stand, divided we fall.

- public entitlements
- wasteful government spending
- taxation

The Tax Foundation estimates that the average American will have to work 102 days to earn enough money to pay his or her 2011 tax obligations at the federal, state, and local levels.

A work year consists of only 261 days, which means that 40 percent of the time we spend working is done to fund some level of government. This clearly indicates that we must work longer and harder just to support the uncontrolled spending habits of our government, particularly its penchant for public entitlements.

Unless deathly ill, true Americans work everyday and when one job is not enough, they take a second or even a third. They don't expect the government to provide for their needs.

Most feel that government should be limited and only concerned with matters that cannot be better handled by the individual states, such as national defense, international trade, and interstate commerce. Size does matter, and in the case of government, smaller is better.

Misapplied and poorly managed entitlement programs have destroyed our cities and rendered affordable housing unsafe. For peace of mind and

God Bless America!

to escape the crime and decay caused by these programs, many have fled to more expensive neighborhoods or into the suburbs where they assume rents or mortgages that strain the limits of their budgets.

Such is the plight of the American middle class. We are hardworking, self-reliant, and prepared to stand our ground—on our own two feet! We are not part of the extreme political left or right. We are simply straight-up Americans, the backbone of this nation, and the majority of the voting population. We still fly the flag, and we know to cross our hearts when the National Anthem is played.

We do not have time to ponder international affairs or other matters that don't affect our daily lives. It's all we can do to keep up with the domestic problems that are constantly created by those in Washington DC.

The current tax system is a mess; paying Uncle Sam his due should not require the use of accountants and attorneys. In addition, only our spending should be taxed, not our earnings and savings. The less we spend, the less we pay, and only necessities such as groceries should be exempt. Herman Cain's 9-9-9 plan sounds pretty good to most of us—it's simplistic and fair to all.

We are happy to pay our part, but it is aggravating to be behind someone in the grocery line who

United we stand, divided we fall.

has three forms of payment: food stamps; WIC; and enough cash to pay for his or her beer, cigarettes, and magazines. To add insult to injury, we must watch as it's all loaded into new, expensive SUVs.

We've worked all week to fill our carts with generic items and potted meat, yet this person who doesn't work eats better than we do. Where's the fairness in our system?

Governing America is a nightmare and more than any one person—or even a body of 535—can understand. Therefore, we try to send only the best to represent us. We depend on you, the government, to ensure that the taxes collected through our sweat and blood are used in a proper and judicious manner. Yet you spend it so liberally.

We may not cause a scene every time we feel that we have been violated, and we do not protest and try to occupy Wall Street, but we still have a voice and the power to bring you down. So please, stand by the principles on which you were elected, and don't forget about those of us in the Middle.

God Bless America!

Chapter 4

Politics and Politicians

Most of the people elected to higher public office would be considered America's elite, having grown up in privileged households before going off to college. They did not start life at the bottom to claw their way up. They became political appointees, academics, "community organizers," and lawyers.

Some jumped right into politics by becoming campaign workers, local politicians, or employees at some level of government.

They have never toiled for any length of time at a sawmill or construction site and have never stood on an assembly line; they taught at the college level, not at a public high school. Their workday consists of staff meetings, power lunches, and cocktails at fund-raisers.

While you are concerned about which bill you can pay or if you'll find another job after you retire, they

United we stand, divided we fall.

concern themselves with whether they should spend the summer at their second home or on a beach in Jamaica.

They don't clip coupons, buy generic, or skip a meal so that the kids can eat. Nor do they service their own cars or even mow their own yards.

Their world is so very different from ours; it is one in which they see only the part that people want them to see, and normally under armed escort. The view from their glass houses within their gated communities must be so peaceful and serene.

Often they are invited to visit communities to see just how successful a federal program has been. The visit is planned weeks in advance and requires the coordination of many people.

First appearances are important, so city workers clean the streets and alleys while the police rid them of problem makers or undesirables. Street lights that have been out for months are repaired, and property owners or tenants are strongly encouraged to make their yards and homes presentable.

On the day of the event, the red carpet is rolled out and the wool is pulled over their eyes. From their perspective, everything is glorious, and the success of the program is obvious. If only they knew or cared enough to drive two blocks over.

Despite all these issues, most people enter politics with an honest desire to serve. They are eager and—much like a rookie cop—feel that they can make the world a better place. But once there, they see how complex, convoluted, and polluted the system really is.

I had the privilege of working with our city attorney, Paul Suskie, in a program that we devised to shut down properties that had become havens for drug dealers, prostitutes, or places of frequent acts of violence.

The program was an instant success, obtaining unbelievable results, and became a catalyst for reclaiming our city.

A strong city attorney is an integral part of the team; he or she must have the fortitude to withstand the political heat and civil litigation that the process entails. Such individuals must be able to do what is right regardless of the personal and political costs.

I did not understand just how rare these characteristics were until later. After all, that's what we expect of all elected officials, right?

Because of our system's excellent results, we were asked to teach it to other cities throughout our own and surrounding states. Naturally, the majority of attendees were law enforcement officers, local politicians, and community leaders.

During our presentations, the police officers got excited seeing all that was possible. Finally they

United we stand, divided we fall.

would be able to help that little old couple who can't afford to move or the single mom struggling to make it on her own. That's why we all became cops to begin with—to be empowered with the ability to help those in need.

As police officers, we know that in most cases, the power of arrest is ineffective; criminals are often released from jail before the cop can complete the paperwork. Once released, the thugs return to the same block, street, and house from which they were arrested and resume their criminal activity.

Because of this, neighbors think the police are not doing their jobs, which leads to distrust in the system; in many cases, the neighbors just give up. After all, why risk filing a complaint if the cops won't do a "dang thing"?

By adapting our solutions to the specific needs of their communities, arrest would no longer be the only option for these police officers; they could now remove criminals from the neighborhoods through the powers of eviction and closure. They could envision life being restored to dying neighborhoods, little kids playing safely in front yards, and criminals getting the punishment they deserved.

By the end of the day, everyone would be pumped up and ready to attack with every resource at their disposal.

God Bless America!

However, within a few weeks of the training, dejected police officers would begin to call—all with the same complaint: the political heat or workload had been too great for their city officials to handle.

Some mayors refused to acknowledge the drug and gang problems within their cities; attorneys cut deals to avoid court, or worse—were asked to back off from certain properties because the owner was a "friend" of a council member.

It sickened me that politics, special interests, or an official's laziness could trump the removal of a drug dealer. This heighted my respect for our city attorney! He was an elected official, and in all the years that we worked together, I never saw him back down to anyone or cater to special interests.

The cries for help from police and community activists never died down, and we felt it was our obligation to find a way to help them.

As a result and through our state representative, we proposed a new state law allowing for the creation of local nuisance abatement boards. Board members would be appointed to a two-year term by the mayor of the city, and these boards would be empowered by the state to take civil enforcement actions against the owners or occupants of nuisance properties. They would have the authority to

United we stand, divided we fall.

evict tenants, levy fines up to $5,000, and order that nuisance structures be demolished, if warranted.

During the legislative session, we received strong support from many members of the House and Senate; each pledged support. However, we still needed approval from the chairman of a particular committee.

During our meeting with the chairman, he made it very clear that we would receive his support only if we could convince other members to support an unpopular bill that he proposed. However, his bill was in no way related to ours and was obviously written with special interests in mind. My head swelled as Paul graciously rose and informed the kind gentleman, "We only need a majority of votes, and yours does not have to be one of them."

I am happy to say that despite the chairman's pledge of no support, the bill passed unanimously and became Arkansas law once signed by Gov. Mike Huckabee. Cities throughout the state use it today.

As you can see, even at local and state levels, it's the people within the system, rather than the system itself, who are the problem. What happened with us here is illustrative of how all levels of government operate.

God Bless America!

When seeking office, politicians promise to put the people's interest before all else, but once elected, some conveniently forget to do so.

In this example, the problems started at the city level and went up from there. Police officers who only wanted to do their jobs were hampered by the malfeasant acts of their elected city officials. From there, it escalated to the state level, where the needs of special interests were placed before the good of the people.

Fortunately, in our case, justice prevailed—but had everyone simply done their jobs to begin with, the enactment of a new law would not have been necessary.

Imagine what it must be like in the hallowed halls of Congress where partisan warfare is regularly waged. When the framers of the Constitution created our bicameral legislature and a separate executive branch, they clearly intended for it to be considerably more difficult to enact legislation than to kill it.

They were resoundingly successful! The legislative processes within the House or Senate alone are extremely complicated and can be painfully slow. But to get a bill successfully through both houses is virtually impossible.

United we stand, divided we fall.

At the time of our founding, this was an excellent idea. Congress consisted of persons who had fought for the creation of a new country and were prepared to defend her principles with their lives. Today, however, many members fight harder for special-interest groups than for the people.

Our founders never envisioned such groups being as influential as they are today. With unlimited financial resources, they have the ability to influence elections; in addition, their influence does not stop on Election Day but continues well into the legislative process.

Representing industry giants, from pharmaceutical research to transportation and everything in between, they are often asked to advise members of Congress on legislation pertaining to their respective industry. Naturally, they will not bite the hand that feeds them, and the information they provide will always be favorable to the industry they represent.

In many instances, they actually author the legislation and solicit support through media campaigns or other means before proposing it to Congress. This is equivalent to having the devil at your doorstep.

The best example of this is the No Child Left Behind Act, which has caused so many problems for our schools and created an uproar among educators.

God Bless America!

The Act is a product of the Business Roundtable—a special-interest group composed of CEOs from over three hundred leading U.S. companies with more than $6 trillion in annual revenues.

Because of its complexity and breadth, few if any congressmen read the Act in its entirety or even understood it. Instead, they were merely briefed on its contents by lobbyists for the Roundtable. Thus, the Act made it through the House with little resistance and no public hearings.

Although it has been such a failure that the Business Roundtable now supports waivers allowing states to opt out of some of the Acts more cumbersome requirements, it still generated up to $5 billion in revenue for many of its member companies.

There is no doubt that the Roundtable had the country's best interest at heart—our children do deserve a better education—but it was also serving the industries it represented.

The No Child Left Behind Act serves as an excellent example of the problems created when the federal government overextends its reach. Education was intended to be a function of the individual states, making it much easier to manage.

The governance of our country is made more difficult for or our elected officials because rather than seeing the world as it really is, they are often

United we stand, divided we fall.

only shown what others want them to see. They are shielded from reality, and sometimes provided with inaccurate information from the people they trust; other times they are simply lied to—just ask President George W. Bush.

The status of their positions separates them from the Middle, and they don't suffer the indignities that we must from the laws that they enact. Most come from privileged backgrounds and have never truly been in touch with average, everyday Americans.

So here is my challenge to 536 of the most powerful people in the world. Go back to your districts, and spend one month in their low-income and crime prone areas.

Leave your staff, bodyguards, and secret service agents in Washington; go alone so that you can see firsthand the mess that has been created. I recommend that you not take your families.

We will provide you with an apartment in the housing projects or a Section 8 home in a surrounding neighborhood. Go smell the blood and hear the screams; see the suffering that your policies have caused.

You won't be able to get back to Washington fast enough, if you make it back at all. But if you do, your heart will be so heavy that implementing the needed changes will be your top priority.

God Bless America!

I understand that you cannot truly do this, but at least read this book in its entirety. Here, the truth has not been cloaked behind political correctness; instead, it has been portrayed in all its glory.

United we stand, divided we fall.

Chapter 5

Idealism vs. Reality

Like most police officers, I entered into service with an honest desire to make the world a better place. I felt it was a noble calling, one in which its members sacrificed of themselves so that peace and order could be maintained.

I could not wait to be a part of the thin blue line that separated good from evil. So, seventeen years ago, I donned my cape, strapped on my bat gear, and set out to save the world.

The day they pinned my badge onto my chest was one of the proudest of my life, second only to the day my daughter came into this world.

When I raised my right hand, I vowed to myself, to my city, to my nation, and, finally, to God that I would protect all citizens just as I would my own family.

Like any rookie cop, I hit the streets full force, thinking I knew it all and that I was well prepared

United we stand, divided we fall.

for the adventure. I was physically fit, eager, and well equipped with all the tools of the trade.

We saved battered women from abusive domestic partners; found runaway children; arrested murderers, rapists, and pedophiles; and exposed ourselves to the very worst that the world had to offer.

We were shot at, spat on, cursed at, hit, kicked, and injured. We saw bodies cut in half, brains splattered onto walls and ceilings, and heard too many last breaths.

We learned to internalize our emotions and to remain calm and stoic while others panicked or were scared or distraught. We hardened ourselves to the horrors of the world.

Our experiences only strengthened our resolve, and we knew that through the pain and horror, we were becoming better defenders of all that is right. Our families could sleep a little safer at night, even in our absence.

Despite our zeal, it didn't take long to see a pattern emerge.

The vast majority of violence, drug activity, and civil unrest occurred in "ghettos," which in its proper meaning, refers to a particularly run-down and destitute portion of a city. Today, however, the term ghetto has been given new meaning by pop-culture, and refers to any portion of a city that consists primarily of "low-income" blacks —good and bad.

During the first few years of a cop's career, these neighborhoods are exciting and are considered choice assignments. But as time progresses and the newness fades, one begins to see the true extent of the damage and severity of the problem.

Portions of these communities have sunken to new lows of immorality, depravity, and slothfulness. Crimes such as prostitution, wife battering, public drunkenness, thievery, drug dealing, murder, and other forms of moral turpitude are considered routine—almost expected behavior.

As a society, we like to take pity on the ghettos' residents and view them as victims of hard luck or as the undereducated who are forced into a life of poverty and crime.

In most cases, that just isn't true. Some (black and white) are hard working and honest and do not want our pity. They are part of America's low-income workforce — a segment of society that we cannot live without. Others, however, are thugs and this is how they choose to live, and they will not change unless forced to do so. This is the portion responsible for all of the bad.

From our exposure to the latter, two primary factors emerged: fatherless children and idle time.

United we stand, divided we fall.

In such situations, there is no family structure, and single mothers—in many cases mere children themselves—are giving birth to fatherless children at astonishing rates.

According to the Heritage Foundation, the out-of-wedlock birth rate for blacks is 72 percent compared to 40.6 percent for whites. Either statistic is bad, but 72 percent is deplorable.

The U.S. Census Bureau reported that 5 million white children and 4.8 million black children lived in so-called poverty in 2010. This is statistically important in that non Hispanic whites make up 63 percent of the population while blacks comprise only 12.6 percent—yet both have approximately the same number of children living in poverty.

Keep in mind that we are dealing with only a very small portion of the black community: the 27 percent classified as living in poverty. The middle and upper classes of the black community are doing very well.

Data recently released by Harvard University's Joint Centre for Housing Studies reported that 48 percent of black families are home owners. The key is that the homeowners are families, and that one simple fact greatly reduces their risk of living in poverty.

God Bless America!

A study conducted by The National Poverty Center revealed that only 6.2 percent of children born into marriage lived in poverty in 2010, compared to 31.6 percent of those born into single-parent households. Despite such irrefutable data, the government continues to offer financial incentives for single mothers to have even more fatherless children.

The other primary factor clearly seen in ghettos was that people simply have too much time on their hands. Too many are not working, and it's not due to a lack of jobs. They choose not to work because they don't have to.

These are persons not counted on the unemployment rolls; they are not actively seeking jobs. These are the people who have never worked or have done so only sporadically. All that they need is provided by an outside source or is stolen.

As law enforcement officers, we are sworn to serve and protect, and society expects us to do just that. We cannot, however, protect you and your property when we are forced to expend the majority of our resources dealing with the problems created by the underclass portions (thugs) of the "ghetto."

These are societal problems and far beyond the scope of law enforcement. With time, it became obvious that our efforts were futile and resulted in little improvement in the community. For every drug dealer, violent criminal, or burglar we sent to prison, ten were in line to take his place.

No matter how much we wanted to do so, we were not going to save the world. We could only try our damnedest to make the best out of a bad situation. Many of us came to the realization, that while we were the defenders of all that is right, the very governments that we served were the creators of all that was and still is wrong.

Chapter 6

The Wise Sage of the Ghetto

One of the most difficult aspects of writing this book was trying not to sound like a racist. The facts do sound bad, and I guess that's the reason the subject has been ignored for so long.

The topics of race-based crime and public entitlements are taboo within the law enforcement community and we dare not speak of them in public. I have received thousands of hours of law enforcement training, and I have never heard the subject broached. It simply is not discussed.

The prevalence of black crime is not just a perception; it's reality. All one must do is read the newspaper or turn on the television to verify it.

It is difficult to openly discuss the topic, and I can't tell you how many times I have written something only to delete it because it sounded like I was

United we stand, divided we fall.

attacking the black community as a whole. Self-doubt erected a wall that my mind could not overcome.

Instead, I decided to venture out, to go "downtown" into some of our worst neighborhoods in search of photo opportunities. I have worked these areas for almost twenty years, and know them inside and out. But I've been there only in uniform, armed, and with backup just a radio call away.

The majority of our homicides occur in these neighborhoods, and the residents are always tense. This is particularly noticeable now, due to a recent rash of murders and shootings.

My first stop is an area just a few blocks from one of our largest housing projects. It's a working-class neighborhood that consists of low paid, hourly wage earners who are very much victims of the ghetto.

Situated between an interstate, a rail yard, and wetlands, the air is filled with an odd mixture of exhaust fumes and stagnant water. The neighborhood of small wood-framed houses was developed during the early-to-middle twentieth century—a time of deep-rooted Southern segregation. This is as far north as "they" were allowed to move.

Despite having its roots in racism, there is a strong sense of community pride which is delicately kept alive by the aging, pre housing projects generation. Tightly knit, when not working, they can often be found socializing under shade trees or front porches. They look out for each other and are very aware of a stranger's presence. I stuck out like a sore thumb and, understandably, drew suspicious stares.

A small group—drinking "toddies" from plastic cups—was seated on the front porch of one of the houses, so I decided to introduce myself and explain my purpose for being there. We conversed politely for a few minutes, but my presence was making them uncomfortable, so I excused myself and moved on.

Down the street, I spotted two shotgun-style houses that I thought epitomized the neighborhood. Next door to these, a burly man in worn jeans and a dirty T-shirt was raking the yard of a well-maintained home. The yard and the home were immaculate, and it was obvious that this was a special place where a lifetime of family memories had been created. I approached the man to ask if I could come onto the property to take pictures of the other houses.

He wanted to know why I needed them, so I briefly explained the concept of the book. He replied, "You gonna tell the truth," and I stated that I would. I guess that I was not believable because he again said, "Nah, man, you gonna tell the real truth."

He removed his glasses and placed the rake onto the ground. I thought to myself, "Oh crap, here we go." He was a big guy—and I mean very big—but

United we stand, divided we fall.

instead of pounding me into the ground, he told me all about the neighborhood and what it was like growing up here.

He introduced himself as Kenneth and explained that this was the house he had grown up in. Born in 1955, he could remember playing as a child on the land on which the housing projects now stand.

His mother had died in this home when he was just a child, and he was raised by his dad, his older siblings, and many neighbors. His dad has since moved to a safer neighborhood, and Kenneth now lives here alone.

By his teenage years, the neighborhood had begun to decline, and cocaine and heroin were prevalent.

The projects were full of young single women, and he was lured in by all of the activity. Before too long, he was "rolling"—making lots of money selling drugs and spending it on his "girls."

He had been to prison twice and was last sentenced to forty-five years. While serving his time, he realized that he had to change or he would die behind bars.

To stay occupied and out of trouble, he voluntarily joined the prison workforce. He was assigned to the kitchen to wash dishes, clean floors, and do other menial tasks. Eventually he was recognized for his hard work and dedication and was promoted to the coveted position of cook, or "prison chef."

It was during this time that he says he found God—as many prisoners claim to do. He said this was a life-altering experience that gave him an inner peace that he'd never before known.

He became a model prisoner and was eventually transferred to the governor's mansion as part of the kitchen staff. His time there was exemplary, and his sentence was commuted.

At the time of our conversation, he had been out for a few years and seemed to be doing very well. He was gainfully employed and a productive member of society. He attended church on a regular basis and worked with neighborhood youth groups in programs designed to keep the kids out of trouble.

I was impressed with his story and had to ask how his life had gone so horribly wrong. He made no excuses; instead, he proudly said that he'd come from a very solid family and that all of his brothers and sisters had done very well. Two had dedicated their lives to military service and were now retired. The others had gone to college and spent most of their lives in the business sector. They, too, were nearing retirement.

He told me that aside from his mother's death, his home life had been as good as anyone's and that his family had been by his side through all of his struggles. The call of the streets had simply been too strong and he had been too weak to resist their temptations.

This wise sage of the ghetto reflected that "the real truth, the one you have to tell, is that there are no families now."

He went on to say that if the lure was too strong for a kid from a family as good as his, just try to imagine how difficult it must be for kids who have no one at home.

Kenneth advised me to tell it from my heart and to not worry about what it sounded like. In a calm and deep voice, he said, "You know this already, but look around. Ain't no white folks here. There more of ya'll on welfare than us, so why ain't none of ya'll here?"

It was simple, he said. "Black folks congregate; ya'll don't." He ended our conversation by saying, "When this many folks of any one race gets together and they ain't been raised by a family and none of 'em work—you're gonna have problems."

When you're not afraid to speak it, the truth really can be that simple. What has taken me almost two hundred pages to write, Kenneth summed up in just a few words.

God Bless America!

Under the current penal system, I am not a big fan of pardons, but I think in Kenneth's case, Gov. Huckabee made the right choice. Truth is, I think God found Kenneth.

Chapter 7

Kenneth's Truth

Despite Kenneth's pleas for me to tell the "real truth," I can't shake the feeling that I must offer a disclaimer.

Many of the most atrocious and sadistic criminals in the nation's history have been white: Al Capone, Machine Gun Kelley, John Wayne Gacy, and Jeffery Dahmer, just to name a few.

Criminals come from all races and socioeconomic classes, but rarely does any other group congregate to the same extent as the criminal element of the black community.

This leads to very public crimes—crimes that are committed on street corners, parking lots, front yards, or other public places. Most people prefer to keep their skeletons in the closet, but persons afflicted with ghetto mentality will expose them without shame to the entire world.

United we stand, divided we fall.

One morning while at police headquarters, I heard a young woman in the hallway screaming for help, so I went to check on her.

Her "man" (meaning her current boyfriend) was in court for beating her up and—not surprising to me, but probably shocking to you—she was there to support him.

While leaving the court, she was approached by her man's "baby-mama," who threatened to kill her. The "baby-mama" was upset because *her* "baby-daddy" had been arrested. *Translated into English, this means that the arrested man's current girlfriend was approached by a woman — the "baby-mama" whom the arrested man "baby-daddy" has children with.*

The victim stated that after the initial confrontation and as she was walking to her car in the parking lot of the police department, her mans "baby-mama" attempted to run her over.

This crime happened in broad daylight in full view of numerous people and in the parking lot of the police department, which should be a safe haven.

While giving the report, the victim stated that this was an ongoing problem; each time she and her man got into it, he would go stay with his "baby-mama". Eventually, they, too, would have a disagreement, and he would come back to her.

God Bless America!

Of course, relationships such as these lead to violence, and the victim showed me a wound on her chest where the other woman had previously stabbed her.

This so clearly illustrates the extent of the problem and just how incapable they are of managing their lives. It's enough to drive a genealogist crazy; men with children from multiple women and women with children from multiple men.

Everything about life is different in the ghetto. The environment has created a new mind-set and the type of person who has defied evolution and somehow devolved.

Morals, compassion, and reasoning have been erased and replaced with violence and aggression. Life carries little value.

Such an environment is so far removed from normality that everyday people of any race find it difficult to comprehend.

United we stand, divided we fall.

Chapter 8

- The Great Divide - White Fears and Racial Leeriness

As a nation, we pride ourselves on the progress we have made in race relations since the days of Jim Crow. We have gone from a state of segregation and white imperialism to a more blended and tolerant people.

For a number of years, minorities have held powerful positions in government, the military, and the corporate world—positions that just a few decades before were reserved for white males.

In 2008, Barack Obama was elected as the first, black President of the United States, the most powerful seat in the world. That same year, the U.S. population was 63 percent non-Hispanic white and 13 percent black.

United we stand, divided we fall.

Although record levels of minority participation were reported, his election would not have been possible without a large base of white support. This alone should put to rest the issue of institutional racism in America.

However, this is not to say that individual biases do not exist. The liberties that we are guaranteed as Americans allow for extremisms as broad ranging as the nation itself. Although we should not always be allowed to voice them, we are entitled to our opinions no matter how radical, disgusting, or socially unacceptable they may be.

We can no more do away with the white supremacist or black radical than we can the political left or right. Fortunately, those who espouse purely racist views, such as David Duke and Louis Farrakhan, are themselves becoming the minority. Their opinions are given credence only by those seeking someone or something to blame for their own personal failure. They are no longer a force in mainstream America and can find support only in the backwoods, ghettos, and prisons.

Although mainstream America has morphed into a more socially advanced and racially tolerant society, it still struggles to understand its new blended identity.

God Bless America!

For various reasons, this often leads to unintentional and sometimes noncognitive bigotry within all racial groups. The degree to which it presents is often determined by socioeconomic and sociocultural factors that are beyond a person's immediate control. For example, the closer someone is economically or geographically to black crime or to those who abuse public entitlements, the more palpable the biases tend to be.

In areas with dense, low-income, black populations, it is rare for there not to be some type of daily accounting of black crime. These are often unpredictable and so heinous and senseless in nature that they send shockwaves of fear throughout an entire community.

Middle- and upper-class blacks are just as fearful of and repulsed by these acts as whites, yet they are often victims of our inability to distinguish between the good and the bad within the black community.

The recognition of skin color and race is part of our normal perception of the world. They are major descriptors and are easily processed by the mind, just as hair and eye colors are. For simplicity, we often categorize people by skin color: brown, white, black, etc. (this helps explain our tendency to racially stereotype). However, such categorization leads to too much emphasis being placed on skin color when attempting to make a distinction between good and bad. Instead, more emphasis should be placed on a person's mannerisms, style of dress, speech, posture, and other signs, as these are much better indicators of someone's intentions.

Generally, street-level criminals of all races stand out from the crowd and are easily recognizable. Most have an air of aggressiveness about them, and their mannerisms are meant to intimidate. Their personal appearance tends to be sub-par, and most appear unkempt and unclean. Typically, the better people present themselves, the less of a threat they are.

Taking all of this into account makes it easier to understand the leeriness that many blacks have toward whites and how they mistake the white communities' leeriness for racism.

Members of all minority groups, whether based on creed, sex, sexual orientation, or any other criteria, are always acutely aware of their minority status—this is particularly true with race.

Other minority classes can alter their appearance or behaviors to minimize their differences, allowing them to blend into most social groups. This is not possible with skin color, nor should it have to be. We must all—black and white—make an earnest effort to unite the good from all races and come together as one nation of law-abiding and peaceful citizens. To intelligently discuss or openly oppose the policies that have done so much damage to our nation is not racist—it's simply something that must be done.

United we stand, divided we fall.

Chapter 9

Black Crime

Black crime is one of the largest and most costly problems faced by our nation. Its impact is widespread and, among other ways, it affects us economically, educationally, patriotically, and emotionally.

As crime increases within a city or town, residents—from the working class to the affluent—flee to a safer community. With such exoduses, cities and counties lose not only their tax bases but also the intellectual, entrepreneurial, and managerial talent needed for prosperity.

Businesses close, factories relocate, and unemployment rises—per capita income declines. Once-thriving school systems become overburdened due to the loss of competitive students, and standardized test scores plummet.

Poverty and desperation set in, drug abuse becomes more rampant, and crime escalates. The remaining residents become infuriated

United we stand, divided we fall.

with government due to the loss of their once-prosperous city and tend to give more complaints than compliments.

This is happening in cities of all sizes across the nation. National discontent is at an all-time high, and many people are preparing for the worst.

For too long, we have downplayed the criminal tendencies of the lower portions of the black community. We attempt to justify their actions by citing factors such as poverty and illiteracy while ignoring the most important factor—personal responsibility.

At some point, we will have to accept that, regardless of the reasons, black crime does exist and that it's becoming ever more violent. Blacks are six times more likely to commit murder and seven times more likely to be murdered than are whites.

These statistics alone are alarming—no one race should have to suffer such terrible losses. However, the fact that it's attributable to such a small portion (approximately 30 percent) of the black population is utterly horrifying; so few people wreaking so much havoc.

The argument is often made that more crimes are committed by whites than blacks. However, viewing crime from this perspective (i.e., without considering that blacks make up less than 14 percent of the total population) does not provide an accurate accounting of the problem. It stands to reason that the population majority will account for a majority of the crimes.

For this reason, crimes should be viewed as a per person average for each race individually. Doing so demonstrates just how much more crime is committed by blacks per capita than whites.

Table 1 represents actual arrests for 2009 as reported by the Bureau of Justice Statistics (BJS). Overall, more whites were arrested in 2009 than blacks —9.5 million and 3.8 million respectively. However, when factored as a percentage of population, the scales tip the other direction. Arrest rates for whites that year were 3848 per 100,000 persons — blacks 9345 per 100,000 persons.

	White	Black	Ratio
Homicide	2.5	15	1:6
Rape	5.7	16	1:3
Robbery	22	171	1:8
Aggravated Assault	108	344	1:3
Burglary	81	229	1:3
Auto Theft	20	71	1:3
Weapons	38	165	1:4
Drug Sales	72	311	1:4
Drug Possession	367	1039	1:3
Violent Crime Index	139	547	1:4
Property Crime Index	474	1248	1:3
Total Arrest Index	3848	9345	1:2

Abnormally high arrest rates for homicide, aggravated assault, robbery, rape, and weapons offenses depict just how pervasive violence is within some portions of the black community. Overall, blacks are four times more likely to be arrested for a violent act than are whites.

Even when faced with such high levels of violence within the black community, many feel that blacks are not to blame. Instead, they claim that blacks are unfairly targeted by law enforcement and that this is what leads to the higher rates of arrest. Accusations such as these, however, ignore two truths.

First—police target criminals and criminals only; large numbers of blacks are arrested because they are committing a large number of crimes.

Second—excluding drug-related offenses, victims are associated with each of the crimes listed above, which prevents law enforcement from using discretion when making an arrest—regardless of the offender's race.

To negate the perceived effects of police or societal biases and to firmly place blame where it belongs, the focus can be narrowed to cities in which no one race has a statistically offsetting majority of the population.

Twenty-two of the nation's one hundred largest metropolitan areas meet this criterion, but not all accurately report crime data to the FBI. Due to the availability of such data, Washington DC, New York City, and Chicago will be used for comparative purposes.

God Bless America!

The racial composition of each of these cities is less than 50 percent white, and all are classified as majority-minority jurisdictions. Blacks and Hispanics account for 60 percent, 52 percent, and 61 percent of the population of each city, respectively.

The police departments for these cities are as diverse as their populations, with minorities making up 48 percent of total sworn officers in NYC and 46.5 percent in Chicago. The majority of sworn officers (58 percent) in our capital city are black, while only 28 percent are white.

With such diversity, the effects of officer-related biases or unfair law enforcement practices should be minimized, resulting in racial and ethnic arrest rates more in line with their population totals.

However, this does not prove to be the case. In 2009, the Chicago Police Department made a total of 181,669 arrests; of those, 164,006 (90.2 percent) were either black or Hispanic.

While blacks accounted for only 33 percent of the population, they were 71.6 percent of all persons arrested. With an equal share of the population (32 percent), whites totaled only 8.8 percent of persons arrested.

As table 2 indicates, blacks were also the majority of persons arrested for all major crimes, with

Hispanics trailing a distant second. Whites accounted for no more than 7.7 percent of persons arrested for any one offense and as low as 2.7 percent for murder.

Table 2	Black		White		Hispanic	
	% of Victims	% of Arrestees	% of Victims	% of Arrestees	% of Victims	% of Arrestees
Murder	75.4	75	3.5	2.7	20	21.7
Robbery	57.4	85.2	17.8	3.5	21.3	10.8
Aggravated Assault	65	68	12	6.6	21.7	23.8
Burglary	52.2	73.7	26.6	7.7	17.9	17.7
Theft	38.7	69	41.1	6.2	16.2	16
Vehicle Theft	50.1	80.2	20.7	5.3	26.8	13.8

Table 2 also allows the data to be viewed from another perspective—that of the victim. The average victim-to-offender ratio for Hispanics is slightly more than 1:1, blacks 1:1.5, and whites 5:1.

This shows that Hispanics are as likely to be victims as they are offenders and may indicate that Hispanic crime is contained within the ethnic community.

Blacks, however, are 1½ times more likely to be arrested for committing crime than they are to be victims of it. The opposite is true for whites, who have a much higher rate of victimization and are five times more likely to be the victim of crime than they are to be arrested for committing it.

God Bless America!

This is not to suggest that blacks are targeting whites. It is only intended to show the effects of black crime on other communities. Excluding murder and aggravated assault, these crimes involve the unauthorized taking of money or property, the victims of which tend to be persons who own property worth taking.

With current data collection methods, it is not possible to separate victims and offenders based on their financial status. However, my professional experiences lead me to believe that if it were, the results would show very similar rates of victimization for middle- and upper-class persons regardless of their race.

Middle- and upper-class neighborhoods are attractive and inviting targets. Because candy is more plentiful there, children from the ghetto prefer to trick or treat in these neighborhoods; criminals prefer them due to the higher abundance and better quality of goods to be stolen.

Conversely, violent crime tends to be intraracial and mostly confined to lower-income neighborhoods.

Nationally, 94 percent of all blacks and 86 percent of all whites murdered are killed by members of their respective races. However, for the interracial portion of homicide, the rate at which blacks

United we stand, divided we fall.

murder whites is eighteen times greater than the rate at which whites murder blacks.

As depicted in table 3, the number of whites murdered in any of the three cities cited was relatively small. Blacks, however, were murdered at alarmingly high rates and were no less than two-thirds of all homicide victims. Washington DC—where blacks are the majority—fared far worse, with 88 percent of all homicide victims coming from the black community.

Table 3	% of Population	% of Homicide Victims	% of Population	% of Homicide Victims	% of Population	% of Homicide Victims
	White		Black		Hispanic	
Washington, DC	39	3	51	88	9	5
New York City	33	5	23	67	29	25
Chicago, IL	32	3	32	74	29	20

Data compiled from the 2010 Annual Reports of the Washington DC and New York City Police Departments and the 2009 Chicago P. D. Annual Report. Population percentages are from the 2010 U.S. Census. These cities reported total homicides of 131, 536, and 461 respectively.

In New York City and Chicago, black homicide rates were 2–3 times greater than their percentage of the population. In all, 95-97 percent of homicide victims in each of these cities were non-Caucasians.

The vast majority of these murders stemmed from black-on-black crime, which has had devastating effects on the entire nation for several decades.

Although murder is the most serious of violent crimes, it is but one indicator of a community's level of violence. On average, for every homicide committed, over fifty felonious assaults will also take place. These assaults include shootings, stabbings, severe beatings, or other attacks that may result in serious bodily injury. Unlike homicide, this category of crime is often underreported in that many prefer to seek "justice" without the aid of law enforcement.

Table 4	% of Victims	% of Offenders	% of Victims	% of Offenders	% of Victims	% of Offenders
Felonious Assaults	White		Black		Hispanic	
New York, NY	13	8	47	55	34	23
Chicago, IL	12	6	65	70	22	22

Only Chicago and New York City reported race statistics for the listed offenses.

As table 4 shows, an overwhelming majority of both victims and offenders of felonious assaults were black. Of particular note, blacks were the only racial group to be offenders more often than victims.

Even though they made up only 32 percent of Chicago's population, blacks committed 70 percent (11,053) of the 15,791 aggravated assaults or batteries that occurred there in 2009. They were listed as victims in 10,264 (65 percent) of these assaults, meaning that most if not all were black on black.

The opposite is true for whites, who had a 50 percent greater likelihood of being victims of aggravated assaults or batteries than offenders.

United we stand, divided we fall.

Unlike the property crimes mentioned previously, these were not crimes directed toward the middle and upper classes.

Experience tells me that many of the white victims of assault, are often low-income individuals living in crime-prone neighborhoods. Others are often persons having cause to enter into these types of areas, such as landlords or people seeking drugs or prostitutes. Additionally, a smaller portion may be attributable to interracial domestic violence in which the offender was black and the victim was white.

While only three cities were used for this analysis, similar results can be found in cities throughout America. Other cities in which the majority of homicide victims are black include the following:

- Milwaukee, WI   73 percent
- Kansas City, MO   77 percent
- Pittsburg, PA   80 percent

Though reductions in black crime must be our primary focus, we should simultaneously implement crime reduction strategies within the Hispanic communities. Currently, their violent crime rates roughly mirror their percentage of the population, however, there is a strong likelihood that these rates will increase if the Hispanic community grows as predicted.

God Bless America!

In a July 11, 2011, article the *Wall Street Journal* reported that the Hispanic population in the United States increased 43 percent since the year 2000, making Hispanics the fastest-growing ethnic group in America. Surprisingly, the majority of the growth was attributed to births rather than immigration.

The article further estimated that 80 percent of the population growth in the United States through the year 2050 will come from immigrants—mainly Hispanics and their children.

In cities such as Los Angeles, California, Hispanics have taken the lead as offenders and account for:

- 65 percent of persons arrested for homicide,
- 53 percent of persons arrested for aggravated assault or battery, and
- 52 percent of persons arrested for robbery.

By and large, law enforcement looks to Los Angeles, New York, and Chicago for emerging trends in criminality. Although it may take several years, new developments in these cities eventually spread to all parts of the nation.

These cities are the birthplaces of the Crips, Bloods, and Folk Nation and have suffered their effects decades before other parts of the country. They are also home to many of the Hispanic gangs

United we stand, divided we fall.

such as MS-13, the Latin Kings, the Surenos, the Mexican Mafia, and others. These gangs are more powerful and better organized than other street gangs, and their members are infinitely more violent. Hispanic gangs are spreading across the nation and already have a foothold in all but a few states.

No matter how bitter the pill may be to swallow, we must take the necessary steps to reduce crime levels within minority communities. We must do so not only to restore the quality of life this nation once offered but also to save our economy, which is collapsing under the heavy weight of crime and the welfare state.

God Bless America!

Chapter 10

The Costs of Crime

The financial burden placed on society in the effort to curtail crime is greater than anyone could imagine.

Direct expenditures by law enforcement at all levels of government increased 155 percent during the twenty-five-year period between 1988 and 2007. Expenditures now total $227 billion dollars a year, 51 percent of which are incurred by local levels of government—your cities and towns.

- Local $116 billion
- State $74 billion
- Federal $37 billion

Cities that suffer the greatest financial burden are those with violent crime rates greater than the national average of just over 400 crimes per 100,000 persons.

United we stand, divided we fall.

In 2009, 264 cities with populations greater than 100,000 persons reported crime data to the FBI, and of those:

- 96 reported less than the national average,
- 103 were equal to but less than twice the national average, and
- 65 were two to five times greater than the national average.

Flint, Michigan, had the honor of being the most violent city in America that year, with 2208 violent crimes per 100,000 persons.

As is to be expected, when crime increases, so does the cost of police services. Typically, the price per citizen for police services in cities with crime rates at or below average is $205. That cost more than doubles to $437 per citizen for cities that are adequately staffed and have crime levels at least twice that of the national average.

The 2010 edition of *City Crime Rankings* listed Colonie, New York, as the safest city in America, with Camden, New Jersey, taking the title of second-most dangerous.

Both have populations of 78,000, yet each citizen of Camden, a city with a violent crime rate thirty times greater than that of Colonie, must pay 4.5 times more for police services.

	Population	Violent Crimes per 100,000	Murders	Police Budget	Cost/Citizen
Colonie, NY	78,003	78	0	$9,000,000	$115
Camden, NJ	78,980	2380	34	$41,747,381	$528

Also on the list of Best and Worst are O'Fallon and St. Louis, Missouri. Though separated by only thirty-seven miles, the quality of life is worlds apart.

	Violent Crimes per 100,000	Murders	Police Budget	Cost/Citizen
O'Fallon, MO	81	1	$11,500,000	$143
St. Louis, MO	2070	143	$128,887,662	$363

St. Louis, the most dangerous city in America in 2010, has a violent crime rate twenty-five times greater than the second-safest city, O'Fallon. As with Camden, the citizens of St. Louis must pay considerably more for police services yet have a much lower quality of life.

As cities struggle with increased costs and lower revenues, maintaining adequate police services becomes more challenging. Police departments typically consume the lion's share of a city's budget and are often the first looked to for reductions.

In response to a recent survey conducted by the International Association of Chiefs of Police, 55 percent of the more than four hundred police executives polled stated "that the new economy presented a serious or severe problem to their agency."

The survey found that 85 percent of respondents had been forced to reduce their budgets during the previous year, with nearly half resorting to layoffs or furloughs of police employees.

The report concluded by saying that we are seeing a "new reality" developing in American policing due to reductions in staffing and services offered.

As financially troublesome as these costs are to cities, they are just the tip of the iceberg and do not include costs for the prosecution, incarceration, and parole or probation of offenders. Nor do they include the costs incurred by victims, insurance companies, hospitals, or intangible costs such as quality of life issues for society in general.

In 2000, *The American Journal of Preventative Medicine* released a study on persons admitted to hospitals as a result of violence-related injuries or deaths.

The study found that total medical costs for the treatment of violence-related deaths and injuries exceeded $7.2 billion when adjusted to 2011 dollars. On average, each death cost $6,578, and each injury $32,000.

God Bless America!

The Centers for Disease Control reported that in 2009, there were 44,466 emergency room visits for violence-related gunshot injuries and 103,635 for stabbings. Using *The American Journal of Preventative Medicine* estimates, these injuries alone cost $4.7 billion.

Since the 1980s, social scientists, economists, and other researchers have conducted numerous studies, attempting to place a dollar-cost value on crime. The most frequently cited studies are Cohen and Rust (2004), French, McCollister, and Reznik (2004) and Cohen and Piquero (2009), all of which have been deemed highly credible.

Although various approaches were used in each study, all attempted to be as cost inclusive as possible. Each considered costs incurred by the government, society, and victims and included lost wages, medical expenses, crime prevention efforts, and so forth.

While these studies used some of the best cost estimation methodologies available, there were notable differences in their final estimations.

To bridge these, the Rand Corporations Center on Quality Policing compiled the results of the three studies and established an average price per crime.

United we stand, divided we fall.

Crime Type	Average Cost
Homicide	$9,394,085
Rape	$236,628
Robbery	$73,070
Serious Assault	$94,750
Burglary	$14,223
Larceny	$2,323

Based on these estimates and data reported to the FBI, the total cost to society in 2009 for just the seven listed offense types was $316 billion. Using similar methods, other researchers have determined that the total cost of all crime exceeds $2.2 trillion per year.

Although such studies cannot establish a definitive cost of crime, they do allow us to see that total societal costs are much greater than that of enforcement only.

Chapter 11

The Ghetto

The ghetto is a harbinger of crime, waste, and gluttony and is supported through government entitlements and fueled by the drug trade.

It's populated by persons accustomed to having all aspects of their lives managed by various state and federal offices and who have contributed very little to their own needs.

Each of us knows the physical boundaries of the ghettos within our cities or towns and the negative effects they have on our lives. Some we see only from a distance; others we must drive through on a regular basis.

They are the places that we warn our children of and tell them to avoid at all costs. When out-of-town visitors come, we provide them with directions for the long way to our homes so that they, too, can avoid the horrors that lie within those neighborhoods.

United we stand, divided we fall.

Built around the turn of the twentieth century, most of these neighborhoods formed around industries plentiful in low-paying, menial jobs. They were segregated communities, consisting of working-class black families just a few generations removed from slavery.

Often, much of the housing was owned by the industry or members of its management. These were company homes that were rented to workers, allowing them to be within walking distance of the factory.

Some of the more prosperous or industrious residents built their own homes from hand-hewn or rough-cut lumber. Just as they are today, these areas were known then as the other side of the railroad tracks.

Ghettos later formed in neighborhoods built between the early 1920s and late 1940s. Prior to their demise, these had been predominately white neighborhoods consisting of young families just starting out in life or those with school-aged children. Here, you would have seen the Bev walking home from school or June Cleaver greeting Ward at the front door.

By the late 1960s, these neighborhoods had begun to show their age; the homes were too small and lacked modern amenities. Families desired larger yards for their children to play in and more space between their houses.

Two-car families were now common, and there was no longer a need to live in the center of the city. Suburbia beckoned, which resulted in new housing opportunities for everyone.

Working- and middle-class black families saw these older neighborhoods as an opportunity to move into areas previously off-limits to them.

These areas would give them the opportunity to pursue their version of the American dream and the ability to provide their children with a higher quality of life.

The civil rights movement was in full swing, and they could envision becoming a fully accepted portion of the nation. They really were "moving on up, to the east side."

While this was an era of prosperity for many, others were becoming increasingly dependent on the government for their livelihoods—particularly their housing needs. This was the portion of black America that had not risen above the obstacles that had been in place for so many years.

As dependency increased, so did the need for centrally located housing. Intended for low-income persons, often without means of private transportation, the housing needed to be in close proximity of government services and community amenities. Someone, somewhere, and for whatever reason decided that these housing needs could best be met within the newly formed working- and middle-class black neighborhoods.

Housing projects were erected and crammed full of people. Rental housing was soon converted to Section 8, and the face of the neighborhood changed.

In what remains of these neighborhoods, you will find elderly couples—both black and white—tightly clinging to their memories. Each day, they touch the doorframes where they recorded their children's lives - inch by inch and year by year.

Here, too, you will find the lonely old veteran tending to the rose garden that his dearly departed wife loved so much. It is his oasis and consists of two metal chairs and a table, all showing their age from the many years of use and exposure. Staked into the ground between the chairs, a faded, hand-painted sign reads: "Our Patch."

Somehow, they block out all of the bad that surrounds them and remain stoic examples of what the neighborhood should have been—not the ghetto it became.

It is estimated that over 60 percent of disturbance calls to which police respond occur within the confines of the ghetto. This shows just how socially defunct the residents have become in that they are incapable of handling even the most basic function of humanity—routine interaction with other people.

As mentioned in other chapters, there will be little improvement until they are introduced to self-reliance.

The ghetto is not just a low-income neighborhood; it is a beast unto itself with its own unique needs and solutions. It's a dark, dirty, violent place, and many of the residents suffer post-traumatic stress disorder like a soldier who has been to war.

It operates twenty-four hours a day, seven days a week—the activity never ends. When driving through, day or night, one is accosted by the stares of persons walking the streets or loitering in vacant lots. There's an eerie presence, and the air is heavy—thickened by the souls of the dead. Persons not from the ghetto are instinctively filled with fear and apprehension as they take in these unfamiliar surroundings.

Plywood, tattooed with gang graffiti, covers the windows of the abandoned, crumbling, neglected houses that line the streets. The occupied houses consist of single mothers, each raising multiple children amid the squalor. These children—often unattended and themselves as neglected

United we stand, divided we fall.

as the housing—play in dirt-covered front yards made bare by the parked cars of the many people who frequently visit. But the horrors that lie beyond many of these front doors are even more appalling.

Several years ago, we were having problems with a small apartment complex in which all of the residents were single women receiving Section 8 housing assistance. Well known as a drug haven, there was a constant flow of vehicular and pedestrian traffic. It had been the site of several shootings, stabbings, and frequent disturbances, but it was a recent homicide that drew our attention in this particular instance.

Due to the propensity for violence, we adopted a zero tolerance approach and arrested everyone for everything. This netted dozens of arrests for felony drug and weapons violations; however, it was but a short-term solution to a long-term problem—nothing we did seemed to slow it down.

The buildings were in terrible disrepair, so we solicited the assistance of our housing code officers, who were able to issue numerous citations to the owner and to several of the residents. In court, the judge could not believe the conditions described and wanted to see them firsthand. I, of course, obliged and drove him to the property.

God Bless America!

The complex consisted of eight duplexes for a total of sixteen housing units. Divided by a city street, there were four buildings on each side of the road. It was obvious even from a distance that this was not a place most people would want to live.

Concrete parking pads, dotted with gang graffiti, were located on both sides of the street, and makeshift barriers of stone and scrap metal were erected to prevent vehicles from driving between the units.

The yards were littered with broken beer bottles, leftover food, and other trash—portions of children's toys rose above knee-high grass. Scattered about were small plastic baggies twisted shut with one end torn off; their contents had already been smoked.

The buildings themselves were even more telling, and nearly every window was cracked or completely broken out. Clear sheets of plastic were draped across to keep the wind and bugs out. Front porches— adorned with worn-out couches and kitchen chairs, served as gathering places for residents.

Entry doors and door frames were heavily damaged, having been kicked in by angry boyfriends or struck with police battering rams. Fly traps hung above them to keep the infestation down.

Though intended to be occupied only by single women and their children, young men loiter around the buildings at all hours. Like most drug dealers, these young men claim to only "stay" at the property and that they live elsewhere, which is not unusual. Most have three or more such places to "stay" while they ply their trade. It is free office space provided by the U.S. taxpayer.

On our visit, the judge was already showing signs of concern, not so much for the residents but for his own safety. Although this complex was only two blocks east of the road he took to work each day, it was as alien to him as another planet.

We made contact with one of the residents, and she granted us permission to enter. The judge was instantly overcome by the horrible smell and pulled his shirt over his nose. Roaches scurried across the floor as we entered the kitchen where last week's meal was rotting on the stove. Mouse droppings could be seen along the baseboards, and flies swarmed the trash can.

As we entered the living room, we noticed an infant sleeping on a floor of worn-out shag carpeting. With each step we took, we heard a crunching noise underfoot, and the judge looked curiously in my direction. Having been there before, I knew the source of the noise and asked that he look for himself.

God Bless America!

The judge bent down, gagged, and ran from the apartment to puke. The noise came from maggots being crushed under our feet as we walked across the carpet on which the baby slept.

This is the ghetto and it is unlike any place you can imagine. It is intentionally kept in a state of chaos and disorder by those who control it—the neglect is just as intentional. It's a battleground, and gangs and thugs know every square inch of it. They know which doors are unlocked, where people stash their guns, and whose houses they can hide in or sell their dope from.

This is their territory, and they own it; the police are mere distractions or hazards of the trade. We're the enemy and are looked upon with anger and disgust. We're shunned, and anyone seen talking to an officer is under immediate suspicion and faces possible retribution.

Although they may fight or flee to avoid it, being arrested is an accepted part of life. Time spent in a city or county jail is but a mere inconvenience, whereas time in prison is an opportunity to gain credibility and become "hood certified."

The residents feed off of each other, and only the strongest survive. When something is needed, they simply take it. It doesn't matter how they get it or who gets hurt. Family members have shot each other fighting over the last piece of pie.

In the ghetto, weakness is fatal, and residents must maintain an appearance of strength. Known as mean-mugging, body language and facial expressions must always convey anger and show a preparedness to fight at a moment's notice. This is a survival tactic — a bluff to avoid a fight because there are no fair fights in the ghetto — someone will get hurt.

They also use intimidating mannerisms to control the streets and to keep strangers out. Generally, groups of three or more take up the entire road and mean-mug you as you try to get by. They know that you will feel threatened by their glares and that if you must pause and inch your way around enough times, you'll stop using that route. Mission accomplished, they continue to own the neighborhood.

This attitude of ghetto mentality is carried with them everywhere they go—schools, parks, department stores, and shopping malls. It has resulted in cities having to assign full-time officers to patrol the hallways of schools and innocent fathers being gunned down in front of their children in the parking lots of local department stores.

God Bless America!

Thugs hope to "own" these places as well and know that because of the chaos and fear they create, we will freely surrender them.

If you've ever experienced the fear, anger, and disgust caused by this mentality, put yourself in the shoes of the good, working-class families who are trapped there and try to imagine how miserable their lives must be.

United we stand, divided we fall.

Chapter 12

The Spread of the Ghetto

By the mid-1980s, the government recognized the complexities, difficulties, and costs associated with government-owned housing projects and sought ways to privatize the system.

Concurrently, and in an attempt to simplify the tax code, broaden the tax base, and eliminate certain tax shelters, Congress passed the Tax Reform Act of 1986.

While increasing incentives to invest in home ownership, the Act also eliminated many of the incentives to invest in rental housing. Once this was realized, many feared it would have a negative impact on low-income persons, as they are more likely to be renters.

With typical misguided reasoning, the government saw this as an opportunity to create affordable

United we stand, divided we fall.

housing for low-income persons in the form of multifamily housing complexes—in essence, privately owned housing projects. This resulted in the creation of the Low Income Housing Tax Credit Program (LIHTC), which was hastily added to the Tax Reform Act.

The program offers tax credits to developers of qualified projects. The developers, in turn, sell the tax credits to investors to offset construction costs.

The investors can then subtract 10 percent of the tax credit—dollar for dollar—each year for ten years directly from their tax liability. This is much better than a standard tax deduction, which only reduces tax liability for one year and only by the amount of the deduction times the investor's tax rate.

In other words, if an investor had deductions of $1000 and was in the 15 percent tax bracket, his tax liability would be reduced by only $150 versus the $1000 tax credit over a period of ten years.

To qualify, a developer must agree to meet certain low-income occupancy thresholds and maximum rent limitations.

For example, a developer could choose to have 40 percent of the units' rent restricted and occupied by households with incomes at or below 60 percent of the HUD adjusted median income for the area. Most, however, choose to impose income restrictions on 100 percent of the units simply because it means they receive more money upfront.

To date, over 2 million housing units have been developed or rehabilitated using funds generated from the program. In 2010, the President's Economic Recovery Advisory Board estimated that the LIHTC Program would cost the United States $61 billion in lost tax revenues for the years 2008–2017.

In addition to the federal tax credit, these properties are also eligible to receive a large portion of the $2 billion in HOME funds that the Department of Housing and Urban Development awards each year.

The HOME Investment Partnership Program is the largest of the Federal Block Grants awarded to states and local governments. Its purpose is to provide decent and affordable housing to low- and very low-income persons. Each state is allotted $3 million in funding per year, while eligible local governments receive a minimum of $500,000.

To top it off, these properties are allowed and even encouraged to accept Section 8 housing vouchers and other forms of housing assistance.

The median rent for tax credit properties in most areas is $650 per month. Generally, someone receiving housing assistance pays a maximum of

30 percent of the monthly rent, which would be $195, with the government paying the remainder.

Under law, the only entities eligible for LIHTC investments are large, widely held C Corporations, not individual investors. Worse yet, should someone with a job and an average income choose to live at such a complex, he or she would have to pay fair market rent.

Everyone wins except the average American. The poor basically live for free, corporate America gets richer, and we continue to pay.

I lived in such a complex prior to its conversion. It was a nice community with long-term residents and low crime. Rarely were the police called to the property, and when they were, it was usually to unlock cars, take a report of someone's vehicle being broken into, or other minor offenses.

The owners opted for a 100 percent income-based conversion, which meant that everyone currently living there had to move. Young and old, black and white, everyone had to go. Even those who had lived there for over twenty years had to pack up and leave.

The entire complex was renovated—all 300+ units. New cabinets, modern appliances, and new windows; the owners spared no expense. After all, it was paid for by the sale of tax credits.

God Bless America!

The investors could claim the tax credits only for occupied units, so banners went up proclaiming "Free Rent," "Free DVD Player" or other enticements. It didn't take long to fill up; we even gained additional population from surrounding cities.

Since then, there has been a huge spike in calls for service to the complex, and crime has increased not only there but in the surrounding neighborhoods. Now, people can be seen loitering in the streets or parking lots at all hours of the day and night; kids fall asleep to the sound of gunshots.

As could be expected, since no one wants to live near crime, those who could move away did so. Many could not sell their houses, so out went the "For Rent" signs.

Originally, the owners attempted to receive full market rent, which resulted in the houses sitting vacant for long periods of time. No one wanted to pay market rent to live near a crime-ridden apartment complex when they could rent a house in a much safer neighborhood for the same price. Of course, rents dropped.

This resulted in a new market of lower-income and Section 8 rental properties. These properties had not yet experienced thirty years of neglect, decay, and crime and were much nicer than previous options. It was like the California Gold Rush in that people could not wait to move there.

When I first hired on with my agency, this was the area of town where rookies dreaded working. It had a very low call volume, had low crime, and honestly—it was boring. Usually only two police officers provided ample service to the community.

Now this patrol area has surpassed all others in call volume and far outpaces other districts in burglaries and other crimes. A typical patrol shift for the area now consists of four to six officers in squad cars and two or more in undercover capacities. Many times, even that is not enough.

The entire appearance of the area has changed. Houses now show signs of neglect in the form of broken windows and peeling paint. Porches are adorned with worn-out couches from which the tenants have unrestricted views of their inoperable cars, parked in their overgrown yards.

This is the ghetto, and it is unlike any place you can imagine. It is intentionally kept in a state of chaos and disorder by those who control it, and the neglect is just as intentional.

God Bless America!

Chapter 13

Root Causes

The issues that we face with crime, education, overpopulation, illegal immigration, middle-class suffering, a bankrupt government, and economy all share one common denominator: public entitlements.

It all started with good intentions: our desire to help those who legitimately could not help themselves; we provided temporary assistance to get them through to better times.

However, through abuses and political maneuvering, the help transformed from temporary assistance into the creation of a lifestyle that has all but destroyed our country. We are well on our way to becoming a fully socialized nation of people dependent on government entitlement programs for their existence.

United we stand, divided we fall.

Merriam-Webster defines entitlement as *a belief that one is deserving of or entitled to certain privileges.* So, as Americans, just what are we entitled to?

One need only refer to one of the most cherished documents of all times to find the answer—the United States Bill of Rights:

Amendment I—Congress shall make no law respecting an establishment of religion, or prohibiting the free exercise thereof; or abridging the freedom of speech, or of the press; or the right of the people peaceably to assemble, and to petition the Government for a redress of grievances.

Amendment II—A well-regulated Militia, being necessary to the security of a free State, the right of the people to keep and bear Arms, shall not be infringed.

Amendment III—No Soldier shall, in time of peace be quartered in any house, without the consent of the Owner, nor in time of war, but in a manner to be prescribed by law.

Amendment IV—The right of the people to be secure in their persons, houses, papers, and effects, against unreasonable searches and seizures, shall not be violated, and no Warrants shall issue, but upon probable cause, supported by Oath or affirmation, and particularly describing the place to be searched, and the persons or things to be seized.

Amendment V—No person shall be held to answer for a capital, or otherwise infamous crime, unless on a presentment or indictment of a Grand Jury, except in cases arising in the land or naval forces, or in the Militia, when in actual service in time of War or public danger; nor shall any person be subject for the same offense to be twice put in jeopardy of life or limb; nor shall be compelled in any criminal case to be a witness against himself, nor be deprived of life, liberty, or property, without due process of law; nor shall private property be taken for public use, without just compensation.

Amendment VI—In all criminal prosecutions, the accused shall enjoy the right to a speedy and public trial, by an impartial jury of the State and district wherein the crime shall have been committed, which district shall have been previously ascertained by law, and to be informed of the nature and cause of the accusation; to be confronted with the witnesses against him; to have compulsory process for obtaining witnesses in his favor, and to have the Assistance of Counsel for his defense.

Amendment VII—In Suits at common law, where the value in controversy shall exceed twenty dollars, the right of trial by jury shall be preserved, and no fact tried by a jury, shall be otherwise re-examined in any Court of the United States, than according to the rules of the common law.

Amendment VIII—Excessive bail shall not be required, nor excessive fines imposed, nor cruel and unusual punishments inflicted.

Amendment IX—The enumeration in the Constitution, of certain rights, shall not be construed to deny or disparage others retained by the people.

United we stand, divided we fall.

Amendment X—The powers not delegated to the United States by the Constitution, nor prohibited by it to the States, are reserved to the States respectively, or to the people.

Nowhere in this document does it state that we are entitled to free food, housing, insurance, or anything else. Nor does it state that we are entitled to a work-free lifestyle in which all of our basic and in some cases more advanced needs are provided for by the government.

An estimated 90 million persons (equivalent to 29 percent of the U.S. population) receive aid through Medicaid, SNAP (food stamps), TANF (welfare), WIC, or any combination thereof. Costs for these four programs in 2009 totaled approx. $531 billion.   In all, the federal government runs over 70 means-tested, antipoverty programs with yearly costs approaching $1 trillion.

Not only are these programs costly to fund, they are also the root cause of many of the problems that our nation faces today. They have led to overwhelmingly high levels of national debt as well as societal division and social discontent. But most notable of all, is that people's dependence on public entitlements has created a lifestyle that has led to unprecedented high levels of crime.

God Bless America!

Although often skirted and tip-toed around, the relationship between crime and the consumption of public entitlements is undeniable. As the following table indicates, states with higher percentages of persons receiving public assistance tend to have higher per capita crime rates.

State	Violent Crime rate	Food Stamp Recipients per Capita	WIC Recipients per Capita	SSI Recipients per Capita	Percent Minority
		Most Violent			
Nevada	702.2	7,569	2,813	1,081	34
South Carolina	670.8	15,073	2,938	1,904	34
Tennessee	667.7	17,027	2,709	2,169	22
Delaware	636.6	10,273	2,669	1,450	31
Alaska	633	9,218	3,868	1,282	33
Louisiana	620	16,111	3,464	3,052	37
New Mexico	619	14,484	3,258	2,142	32
Florida	612.5	10,532	2,750	1,675	25
Maryland	589.9	7,969	2,594	1,376	42
Arkansas	517.7	14,229	3,425	2,990	23
Oklahoma	501.1	12,826	3,607	2,063	28
Illinois	497.2	11,327	2,380	1,625	28.5
Michigan	497	14,547	2,582	2,057	21
Missouri	491.8	13,376	2,526	1,821	17
Texas	490.9	12,118	4,181	1,711	30
California	472	7,225	3,949	1,921	42
Massachusetts	457.1	9,519	1,905	2,072	19.6
Alabama	449.8	14,423	3,079	2,943	31.5
Georgia	426.1	13,084	3,174	1,735	40
Arizona	408.3	12,341	3,135	1,227	27
		Least Violent			
West Virginia	296.5	16,813	2,846	3,748	6
Nebraska	281.6	7,437	2,520	1,149	14
Mississippi	281.3	17,138	3,463	3,306	41
Iowa	279.2	9,811	2,483	1,321	8.7
Hawaii	274.8	8,848	2,859	1,219	16.4
Kentucky	258.7	16,267	3,224	3,634	12.2
Wisconsin	257	9,689	2,238	1,550	13.8
Oregon	254.7	15,188	2,984	1,459	16.4
Montana	253.6	9,482	2,127	1,448	10.6
Rhode Island	252.6	9,713	2,424	2,330	18.6
Minnesota	243.9	6,551	2,631	1,237	15
Idaho	228.4	8,814	3,043	1,451	11
Wyoming	228.2	4,917	2,515	988	9.3
Virginia	226.8	8,268	2,035	1,397	31.4
Utah	212.7	6,654	2,707	801	14
North Dakota	200.7	8,204	2,260	1,009	10
South Dakota	185.6	9,107	2,804	1,296	14
New Hampshire	159.6	5,960	1,351	1,116	6
Vermont	131.4	11,600	2,703	1,958	5
Maine	119.8	15,266	2,060	2,223	5

God Bless America!

Data compiled from the Federal Bureau of Investigations, the Social Security Administration, and the United States Department of Agriculture and is for the year 2009. The category for SSI only includes persons younger than age 65.

The adjacent table lists, in descending order, the twenty states with the highest violent crime rates and the twenty states with the lowest, their respective rankings for Food Stamp, WIC, and SSI consumption as well as each states percentage of minority population. (Shading indicates that the state also ranked in the top twenty among states for that particular category).

Of the twenty *most violent states*, sixteen were also among the top twenty states with the highest number of recipients in at least one of the three other categories (Food Stamps, WIC and SSI). Additionally, thirteen were among the top twenty of states with the highest number of recipients in two of the other categories and six states were among the highest in all three.

Of the twenty *least violent states*, two ranked in the top twenty of states for two of the other categories, while three ranked in all three categories. In total, *only 9* of the twenty least violent states ranked in *any* of the other categories.

It does not take statisticians and complex mathematical equations to determine if a relationship exists between crime and public entitlements. Although there are some anomalies, the relationship can be established just by comparing the amount of shading used in the section for the most violent states, to that used in the section for the least violent states. As the violent crime rates decrease, so too do the rates at which people are dependent on public entitlements for their survival.

In addition to establishing the crime-entitlement relationship, the data also indicates that a relationship exists between minorities and crime. Of the twenty most violent states, 15 were among the twenty states with the highest minority populations while that was true for only two of the least violent states. This fact may be more indicative of the social differences (Ghetto mentality) between low-income blacks and low-income whites, than it is differences between whites and blacks in general.

As an interesting side note, the Robert Wood Johnson Foundation produced a list of the twenty states with the highest rates of childhood obesity and eleven, of the twenty most violent states were included. Not surprisingly, only four of the least violent states shared this distinction.

While many factors are associated with childhood obesity, parental neglect and an over abundance of cost-free food cannot be discounted. Not having to shoulder personal financial responsibility for their offspring allows the "impoverished" class of American society to grow without constraint, while the working and middle classes shrink. This reduces the number of people paying taxes and the burden to pay for entitlement programs is being placed on an increasingly smaller portion of the population.

The Internal Revenue service reported that 45 percent of U.S. households owed no federal income taxes in 2010, up from 39 percent in 2005. Were we not operating in deficit mode, the liability to each *taxpaying* household to fund these programs would be $15,577.

As of 2011, the U.S. Federal debt was $15,476,000,000,000.00 ($15.4 trillion). That's a lot of numbers! I can remember as a kid using trillion to exaggerate something just as we would with gazillion. It seemed like a make-believe number that no one could imagine, yet now we must enumerate it.

While the average American family earns only $49,445, every household member's portion of the national debt is more than $50,000—man, woman, and child. Government spending has caused us to become the most debt-laden generation in history, yet Congress can only agree on a 1 percent reduction in federal spending ($38.5 billion).

United we stand, divided we fall.

For more clarity, the country's balance sheet can be compared to a family's budget by removing the last eight digits.

U.S. Tax Revenue	$2,302,000,000,000
Federal Budget	$3,834,000,000,000
New Debt	$1,532,000,000,000
National Debt	$15,476,000,000,000
Recent Budget Cuts	$38,500,000,000
Familiy Income	$23,020
Family Budget	$38,340
New Family Debt	$15,320
Outstanding Balance	$154,760
Budget Reductions	$382

With reductions in spending of only $385, this family will never be able to overcome its debt of more than $150,000. The same applies to the nation.

To achieve the needed levels of reductions, we must all be willing to share some of the pain. However, no one should feel it more than "entitled persons"—those whose only means of support comes from taxpayers. This does not include the elderly who have worked and paid into Social Security and Medicare or the truly disabled. The elderly have earned it, and the truly disabled need it.

God Bless America!

Originally, I intended to go into great detail about all of the entitlement programs that people use to suck America dry, but I rapidly became overwhelmed—not only by the sheer number of programs available but by the complexity of trying to find complete and accurate information.

I really doubt anyone knows exactly how much we spend supporting other people except perhaps the president and a few of his closest advisors. There is some speculation about the existence of a President's Book of Secrets, and the answer may be contained therein. If so, it would help explain why all presidents age so drastically once in office.

Regardless of the actual costs, we have expanded entitlement programs far beyond their original scope, and the American people have had all that they can stand.

Americans are a kind-hearted and generous people by nature, and most would give their neighbor the shirt off their back if deserved. We give billions of dollars each year to various charities and donate an untold number of hours to charitable work.

This, however, is something that we choose and want to do—it is not forced on us. Most Americans do not like having portions of their earnings and savings seized through taxes, which are then doled out to the chronically disadvantaged.

United we stand, divided we fall.

There will always be persons in need of assistance due to unexpected events such as job losses, short-term illnesses, or downturns in the economy. As individuals and as a nation, we should temporarily extend a helping hand, but only if those receiving assistance are prepared to take the steps necessary to wean themselves from the government dole.

We should also be prepared to financially stand behind those who may have difficulties supporting themselves, such as the elderly or persons with *legitimate* medical conditions.

In the city that I police, we have a man known to everyone as "Crazy Carl." He suffers a multitude of mental illnesses and walks the streets daily—often with his pants down to his knees and his private parts exposed. Normally, he will be engaged in very animated conversations with nonexistent people; his arms flailing about as he speaks to them. His behavior is very alarming and disheartening, and many people call 911 to report it every day.

He is harmless, and the courts have ruled that he is fit to live freely because he is not a danger to himself or other persons. However, because of his disabilities, he must suffer the physical, financial, and other types of abuses inflicted on him by the dredges of our society.

God Bless America!

As police officers, we really can't do much for him within the *injustice* system; his crimes are minor, and he can't be jailed due to overcrowding. He needs to be placed into a home that will ensure that he receives the medication and care he needs.

Instead, he receives disability, food stamps, and other forms of assistance. His physical care and the management of his daily life are provided by so-called friends who live with him in a home for which he receives housing assistance.

Despite receiving public aid, he looks and smells worse than a homeless person. His clothes are nothing more than ragged hand-me-downs that are literally rotting off his back. His "care-takers" are only taking care of themselves, surviving off the housing, food, and cash that we the taxpayers provide for Carl.

Naturally, we all take pity on him, and it is not uncommon to see police officers take him his favorite lunch of a big burrito and a 7-Up. We look out for Carl because no one else will. He is trapped between the judiciary's duty to protect individual rights and the state's obligation to care for the incompetent.

As an innocent casualty of this battle, he has been abandoned by the persons and systems intended to guide him through the foggy haze of his mental

United we stand, divided we fall.

illness. Alone and confused, he must now navigate the complex maze of the often abused welfare state.

As with Carl's "care-givers" there will always be pitiful excuses of human beings lurking in plain sight, waiting to abuse whatever assistance is offered. It has become a lifestyle for many, and they are very capable of manipulating the system to their advantage.

I recently had the displeasure of becoming involved with one of the most disgusting examples of such abuse that I've ever encountered.

It involved a man from out of state who was attempting to locate a daughter whom he had sired with a woman whom he thought now lived in our jurisdiction.

He'd heard that the daughter, now age thirteen and with whom he'd never had contact, had given birth to a child of her own. His children by his current "wife" were grown, and they were no longer receiving financial assistance for them.

He was of the opinion that because his "baby mama" had received thirteen years of financial assistance for his child, he should now receive it for the grandchild. His plan was to have the daughter either come live with him or have her place the child into his custody. Fortunately, this was a civil matter, and I was not able to provide him with any assistance.

God Bless America!

We have long desired to help those less fortunate than ourselves. We were just too naive to believe that our kindnesses would be abused to the extent that they have been.

With the 1969 release of *In the Ghetto*, Elvis Presley captured the very essence of America's empathy for the poor and how we, as a nation, falsely accepted blame and responsibility for the problems they created for themselves. If available, take a moment to listen to the song. It still brings me to tears.

The lyrics concern a single mother that has just given birth to a new child. She's crying, "Cause if there's one thing that she don't need, it's another hungry mouth to feed, In the Ghetto." He goes on to describe how it's the nation's responsibility to provide for the child so that he doesn't grow into an "angry young man someday."

With uncanny accuracy, he tells of the child growing up hungry and neglected. Just as some children today do, this child turns to the streets for survival, where he "learns to steal and how to fight." As can be expected, the young man dies after being gunned down for stealing a car, and as "his mama cries" over his dead body, the tragedy begins anew in yet another 'family': "On a cold and grey Chicago mornin', another little baby child is born In the Ghetto...and his mama cries."

United we stand, divided we fall.

Fast-forward to 2004, and the release of the rap version of *In the Ghetto* by Busta Rhymes. While Elvis' version evokes feelings of sympathy and compassion, this modern rendition evokes only anger and disgust.

As a warning to outsiders, the song starts with "if you ain't from the ghetto, don't come to the f_ _king ghetto." The 'singer' then takes the listener on a guided tour and offers a vivid depiction of young life in the hood. He describes himself as being "Dumb and oh so lazy," — "selling drugs in front of Pancho Deli," where "crackhead chicks still smoke with babies in they belly."

The entire song speaks of drugs, crime, and other antisocial and antihuman behaviors. It shows the level of respect held for criminals and the level of disrespect held for society, its rules, and those who must enforce them, "We honor the code of the street and live by the rules, in the ghetto."

Even as a semi successful adult, he is inextricably connected to the life "You can take me out the ghetto, but you can't take it from me – Gotta love it!"

By now, it should be painfully obvious to us all, that the helping hand Elvis first asked us to extend forty-three years ago, not only failed to prevent that hungry, young boy from growing into an "angry young man" it transformed succeeding generations

God Bless America!

into "lazy," drug dealing thugs that were, and still are "looking for trouble" while "hanging out on corners" with nothing to do with their time, and now… a nation cries.

We are not a third-world country accustomed to extreme suffering. Therefore, none of us wishes to see any child roaming the streets hungry. But its time that we wake up and see, that the "helping hand" we extended, has caused more harm, than good. At some point, personal responsibility must come into play. These children are not conceived accidentally—they are paychecks and a means of obtaining prestige.

Young girls, unable to even support themselves, purposefully seek out the alpha thugs within their environments to sire their out-of-wedlock children. In return, they receive a level of safety, the respect of their peers, and credibility on the streets.

The financial incentives that we, as a society, offer these girls not only support out-of-wedlock births but encourage the continuance of such immoral behavior. In return for our misplaced kindness, these single-mothers produce:

- 70 percent of juvenile inmates serving long sentences
- 72 percent of all juveniles arrested for murder

United we stand, divided we fall.

- 60 percent of rapists
- 70 percent of teenage births, dropouts, suicides, runaways and juvenile delinquents
- 80 percent of all prison inmates
  According to the Index of Leading Cultural Indicators

Despite these facts, we continue to allow them to birth as many babies as their young bodies can withstand. Each year, Medicaid pays for the births of nearly 2 million children, most of which are born to single mothers. With an average price of $11,000 per birth, total costs to taxpayers will soon exceed $20 billion per year.

It should be common sense that if you can't pay for your child's birth, you will not be capable of supporting them for the next 18+ years. However, these girls don't have to worry about this—they know that taxpayers will be forced to step in and do it for them.

It is important to note, though, that if these girls are physically healthy enough to give birth, they are also physically healthy enough to work. There are plenty of strong, single moms doing just that and more today.

Some people claim that these girls or young women do not have the skills or education necessary to find or retain employment. But just how much education does it really take to push a broom, take out trash, or clean tables? None.

God Bless America!

To avoid being a burden on society, many Americans with no more than high school diplomas or less toil at laborious jobs each day. This should be the standard for all people: earn what you get, and fend for yourself.

There are plenty of jobs available; some people are just too lazy to take them or know they can receive more money through entitlements than they could earn. Were these jobs not available, we would not have the problems that we do with illegal immigrants. They are not coming here for the weather!

They are willing to leave their homelands to take the jobs that some Americans would never consider doing. Why bother working though, when you can have twenty-four hours a day of free time, and still be given everything that you need to survive.

The answer to that, is simple. If for no other reason, one should work, to stave off boredom. Everyone needs some degree of excitement in their lives, and most get it through the challenges of their job, winning a round of golf, or participating in their children's athletic or academic events. None of this exists for thugs in the ghetto.

They, of course, don't have to work, traditional families are nonexistent, and most can't tell you their kids names, much less where their schools are located.

United we stand, divided we fall.

They turn to the streets for their excitement, and it is plentiful. There is no life more exhilarating than that of a street-level criminal—it's a constant adrenaline rush. They must be ever vigilant, know their surroundings, and be aware of who may be coming for them—because someone always is.

Each encounter with danger brings feelings of euphoria and invincibility and heightens their senses. At that moment, everything seems more vivid: sounds, smells, colors. Their bodies tense, and it feels as if their muscles are ripping through their skin. They feel strong and powerful because they survived!

The rush is a drug and just as addicting as cocaine. Once you have tasted it, you'll always crave it.

Police work is often described as 90 percent boredom and 10 percent sheer terror. We, too, are addicted to the rush and live for that 10 percent of the time. However, police are taught to control the rush and how to contain themselves. Thugs aren't, and that's why they're so dangerous.

They'll get the rush the first few times they stick a gun in someone's face to rob them. Eventually, even that will become routine and boring, and the next time, they'll escalate the violence.

Combine their craving for the rush with the intense high from crack cocaine, and you have a

God Bless America!

monster—one raised by the streets, without morals or compassion, and with very little emotion. Just as Busta Rhymes described, these types of people are "soldiers" of the ghetto "with a different state of mind" who've been raised to "take it if they want it" and that "money comes quicker doing crime."

This is what we have created by ensuring that generation after generation does not have to work to support themselves and their families. People have far too much time on their hands, and that almost always leads to trouble.

Money is not the solution. Directly or indirectly, we provide thugs with everything that they need to survive, yet they still commit crime. It has nothing to do with survival or putting food on the table. It's a mind-set and a lifestyle, and we have to stop supporting it.

This mind-set is passed from one generation to the next, with each becoming progressively meaner and even more dependent. I shudder to think just how evil and corrupt the next generations will be.

United we stand, divided we fall.

Chapter 14

The King and His Soldiers

Every ghetto has a king—an overseer of the criminal underworld. Shrouded in the pain and suffering of others, the title means that the bearer has proven to be the most violent and street-smart of all contenders. It's an honorific that only a few will earn, and fewer still will survive.

Law enforcement is a unique profession—one that requires its members to stand witness to the carnage caused by thugs attempting to climb the hierarchical ladder of the criminal underworld. For most, it is a short climb, and whether directly or indirectly, their rise is usually halted by either death or incarceration for the deaths they've caused.

Personally, I've known only one to beat the odds of death or long-term imprisonment long enough to be crowned king of the ghetto. Though on opposite

United we stand, divided we fall.

sides of the fence, our careers began in the same era, and our paths crossed several times throughout the years. We learned each other's ins and outs from the ghetto's version of the game cat and mouse. I learned to recognize when he was holding dope, and he learned to recognize when I knew it. He would flee but never fight.

We'd grown to respect each other as only cops and thugs can, and when it was safe for him to do so, we engaged in guarded but personal conversations. Despite hating what the other stood for, I think we both enjoyed our discussions.

Covered in gang tattoos and built like a power lifter, he was quietly spoken and very personable. He claimed to be a businessman just trying to make a living and felt that he had been unjustly labeled a criminal. He claimed to live by the rules of the ghetto—not the laws of society.

To fully understand his definition of a "businessman," we must look back several years, to the days prior to his first prison sentence. During the turbulence and violence of the mid-1990s, he, along with his father and a brother, were kingpins of the drug trade, and he amassed a small fortune.

He owned several houses and a fleet of customized SUVs, Cadillacs, and sports cars—none of which could be traced back to him. However, his most prized possession was a 24-karat gold medallion shaped to form the initials of his street name.

The total weight of the medallion was 2.2 pounds, or 1 kilo, and valued at over $52,000. Its weight signified his participation in the drug trade, and its value signified his success. Upper-level drug dealers move only large quantities of a kilo or greater.

He had never spent a day of his life gainfully employed but managed to live like a rock star. Doesn't take a genius to spot a drug dealer! Eventually his flamboyance and cavalier lifestyle caught up with him. He was arrested and sentenced to thirteen years in one of our well-appointed federal penitentiaries—but served less than five years.

Upon his release, he assumed his former role as a major drug trafficker and expanded his "business." It flourished to the point that he could no longer hide his vast sums of ill-gotten gains—too much cash was accumulating, and it needed to be cleaned.

He became an urban investor—a venture capitalist of the ghetto—and financed many aspiring rappers, music producers, and other artists. With no paper trails and with their lives as collateral, he funded numerous "hood-certified" businesses.

Eventually he opened and managed a large and relatively successful nightclub of his own, and it attracted his caliber of people.

United we stand, divided we fall.

Located in the heart of the ghetto and open only on weekends, the club was an after-hours hotspot for thugs. Most nights the lines to get in wrapped around the building and often overflowed into the streets.

From the night it opened, the club was problematic. Frequent fights, shootings, and a murder brought the club under police scrutiny, and soon it was permanently closed.

The closing of the club was but the beginning of his problems. People were looking for him, and he forgot to watch his back. One night, he was lured out of his home by people whom he must have trusted, and he was gunned down on his own front porch— one shot to the back of the head.

Word of his death spread quickly, and the ghetto began to mourn. Although his acts of benevolence and seeming desire to help others were but ruses to hide his illegal gains, people were still appreciative, and he became a martyr.

They wore T-shirts emblazoned with his picture, and signs of morning were posted at businesses he'd supported. Most significant was an image someone posted to Facebook.

The photograph had been altered, and he appeared to be an angel with wings on his back—

God Bless America!

standing before the Pearly Gates. A caption above the photo read "King of the Ghetto."

His obituary stated that he left behind his wife and five children as well as fifteen brothers and sisters and that he was preceded in death by a younger brother who'd been gunned down a few years earlier...*and his momma cries.*

Under different circumstance, he could have been so much more than king of the ghetto. Instead, he chose to remain a product of his environment and became just another statistic.

Based on the dynamics of the family, it is safe to assume that most, if not all, of his siblings have led less than productive lives. Their fates were predetermined by the unrighteous union of a thug and a welfare queen.

Their father, a notorious drug dealer with whom they never lived, encouraged and actually solicited their participation in his criminal activity. Meanwhile, the mother was nothing more than a baby factory and either had her hands too full with kids or just didn't care enough to shield them from the father's criminal influences. They are an entitlement family.

Assuming Medicaid paid for the births of each of these children, this one family cost the U.S. taxpayers

$187,000—not counting any other entitlements they may have received.

The king had five known children. If each of his sixteen siblings miraculously placed the same limitations on their own contributions to the national population, the tab just for birthing that generation would be $935,000.

Some children, like the "king," are inducted into a life of crime by their parents, while others are pushed aside to fend for themselves. Children from families as large as the one I have mentioned have no one in their lives to see to their needs. They are lost souls from the day they are born.

Drive through any "low-income" area, and you'll see diaper-clad babies barely old enough to walk playing in the streets with no adult supervision. From the day they first come home, they are exposed to the worst horrors the world has to offer.

They become wards of the streets, where they will develop their "survival instincts and hustle." All children need love, attention, and protection. When it is not available at home, they will find it from whatever source is willing to provide it. Most turn to gangs or quasi-gangs.

They'll develop loyalties to their gang and to the streets, which they'll defend with their lives. They'll be soldiers of an army whose recruits are children and whose leaders are thugs. Starting at the bottom, they will serve as lookouts or will hold dope for older members.

Beginning with petty larceny, they'll be taught to steal before they graduate to the more serious crimes of burglary and robbery. Once they've proven themselves and put in their time, they'll be promoted to the coveted rank of a dealer.

Now they have earned that which they have always craved: respect and fear from others. In doing so, they have entered into the most dangerous part of their young lives.

No longer are they victims of the chaos and violence within the ghetto; they are now the source. Eventually, the hour of their demise will be time stamped within the pages of a police blotter. Here is an example of one such story.

10:52 a.m. "caller advises her cousin has been shot."

Police respond to a run-down, 1930s-era, brick bungalow. Several inoperable cars are parked in the front yard, and from the height of the grass, it appears they have not been moved in several months. Between the cars lie ruptured garbage bags from which the stench is overpowering.

United we stand, divided we fall.

As we approach, the shooter instantly surrenders and is taken into custody. Afterward, we enter the home to render aid to the victim. Inside, we find the body of a young black male with a single bullet hole to the right side of his head.

Just twenty-three years old, he is well known to all of the officers on scene. He is a drug dealer, burglar, and all-around thug; his street name is "Dum Dum" (*though it has the same meaning, this is a modification of his real street name*).

At an age in which most are just starting life, this young man dies in a roach-infested and filthy battle-field, grasping a bag of crack cocaine.

Paramedics arrive on scene and determine that he has passed and that it would be futile to render any type of aid. Of course, we could tell that just from the blood splatter.

In compliance with the Supreme Court's opinion on searches, we exit the home, leaving the body on the floor to begin the laborious process of obtaining a search warrant to complete our jobs.

We string yellow tape to secure the crime scene. It's a new brand of tape, and we all joke about the image of "Officer Friendly"—smiling and with his arm extended as if politely asking people not to cross the line. This will surely keep the pained and angry family members and friends at bay.

God Bless America!

Already a crowd of thirty has gathered, and many are using their cell phone's video camera to record the event. Scenes such as this typically turn into a "ghetto block party" and can quickly overwhelm the police.

Within minutes, more vehicles are pulling onto the street; the occupants are screaming "Oh Lord," "Aw, hell; naw, they didn't have to kill him," "What's wrong with these nigga's?" or other such phrases as they rush the crime scene.

Before long, the crowd exceeds fifty, with most gathering around the crime scene tape while other groups form on porches or under carports.

We are on high alert—panning the crowds to interpret body language and listening to conversations that may indicate trouble. Tension has been brewing in the "hood" for weeks due to a recent, justified officer involved shooting. Threats have been made to "take out a cop," and more are heard today; somehow, we are to blame for this shooting as well.

We have only six officers present, and it's not enough to preserve the crime scene and control the crowd—we call for backup.

A thunderstorm develops, and heavy rains begin to pour down. We quickly don our rain gear, but it does no good; within minutes, we are soaked to the bone.

United we stand, divided we fall.

It's just another day in the hood: cops standing in the rain, earning our paychecks so that we can pay taxes only to support all of these able-bodied people who are amassing around us. It's the middle of a workday, and somehow this one small street can attract this many people.

As a public servant, I am faced with the fact that I will work until the day I die, yet all of these people are able to retire at birth.

By now, the crowds have grown so large that we have given up all hope of keeping track of them; the entire street is lined with people.

It sounds as though a celebration is occurring, with people laughing and joking among themselves. Members of the victim's family still stand by the tape, the anger and pain clearly visible on their faces. The scene is almost reminiscent of an honor guard paying tribute to a fallen soldier or police officer.

The victim's cousin is being comforted by a young female when I hear him state, "He died for the hood." This is the type of soldier Busta mentioned in his song—not an honorable defender of the nation but a crack-dealing thug bent on destroying the very neighborhood in which he lives.

It's an ironic scene: inside lies the dead body of a young man, face down in a pool of blood. While

God Bless America!

his family stands vigilant, others act out in an almost carnival-like atmosphere, even in the pouring rain.

Shaking off the image, I wave to a child barely old enough to walk, and as he waves back, the mother slaps his hand. God forbid the child should view an officer as anything other than the enemy.

A family member rushes the crime scene in an attempt to cross the tape and must be restrained by an officer. This inflames the crowd, and the tension becomes even more palpable. People begin screaming and cursing at us for laying hands on the poor, sad soul they claim was merely venting his anger.

As officers, we know that we are preserving evidence so that the perpetrator may one day be brought to "justice." They couldn't care less about justice and want only vengeance.

Threats are already being made, and we overhear someone say, "This shit ain't over; hell, naw, it ain't even started yet. That nigga's house gonna burn." We know ghetto justice will be served, and the cycle will once again repeat itself.

Finally, after three hours, the search warrant is received, and our detectives enter the home to process the scene. The crowd pulls nearer, and more cameras appear in anticipation of the body being rolled out.

United we stand, divided we fall.

These images will be uploaded instantly to Facebook and other social networking sites to spread the news of what has happened. In contrast, my daughter uploads pictures of her dog or the places she has been with her friends. What a difference in lifestyles.

The victim's mother, who could be a poster child for all that is wrong with society, loses her composure as her young son, wrapped in a body bag on which his blood is visible, is rolled out by the coroner.

She drops to her knees and releases a soulful and agonizing wail, causing the crowd to react. Small fights break out between family and friends of the victim and those of the suspect.

I quickly escort the mother down the street, away from all that is occurring. She collapses into my arms, and someone informs me that this is her second son to have been killed in a month's time. As I hold her, I can't imagine her pain or even living such a lifestyle.

Everyone is worried that I will arrest her, as she keeps trying to go back to where her son had been. In reality, I just want her to go home so that she doesn't have to see any more of this.

His obituary states that he leaves behind two children, neither of which shares his last name, and ten brothers and sisters with five different surnames.

God Bless America!

...and his momma cries.

For a moment, set your sympathies aside—don't think about the personal suffering and tragic loss of life. Focus instead on the actual monetary costs associated with such incidences and the strains they place on the cities in which they occur.

The investigation of this one incident required an on-scene presence of:

- 10 police officers, 9 police cars
- 3 firemen, 1 fire truck
- 2 paramedics, 1 ambulance
- 6 detectives, 3 cars
- 2 detectives in a crime scene van
- 2 coroner investigators, 1 van
- 1 deputy coroner, 1 car.

Additionally it required two detectives to write the search warrant and a judge to approve it. An officer had to transport the suspect to the Detectives Division where the suspect was interviewed by two more detectives with a detective supervisor monitoring the interview.

This is just the initial response and does not include the dozens of man hours the lead detective will log in the future or the time spent by the prosecuting attorney's office, the jail staff, and eventually, a judge and jury.

United we stand, divided we fall.

Ten uniformed officers were required to secure this one scene, and on a good day, my department can field 14–16 officers per shift. This leaves a maximum of six officers to police a city with a population of 60,000. And you wonder why the police cannot protect your property.

Thousands of dollars will be spent by the crime lab conducting an autopsy, analyzing the weapon, performing DNA tests, and so much more. The state will pay for the victim's funeral, and more than likely, the victim's family will receive other monetary assistance through the state's Victim Assistance Program.

This is a scene played out hundreds of times each day all throughout this great country of ours. As taxpayers, we paid for the prenatal care received by this young man's mother, his birth, and twenty-three years of medical care, education, housing, food at his home and school, numerous incarcerations, probations, the investigation of his death, and finally, his funeral.

To compound the problem, we are doing the same for the multiple women with whom he has had children, and those children are likely to be just as costly as he was.

I would venture to guess that more money was expended to get him to this point in life than what

God Bless America!

we as taxpayers spent on our own children. As callous as this may sound, I feel that this is a bad investment and that we should consider changing our broker...politicians.

All of this to service someone who has spent his life wreaking havoc on society and who has been a recipient of government entitlements since birth. Just in the span of his short life, he was mentioned in fifteen police reports and arrested eleven times.

Some of you reading this will feel sorry for "Dum Dum" because he grew up poor and "had to resort to crime to survive." But that simply is not true.

Many recipients of public entitlements have more money handed to them with no more effort than walking to the mailbox than many hard-working Americans earn in a year.

In addition, being poor does not mean that one has to resort to criminality or immoral behavior. I come from a family of Mississippi sharecroppers, and my daddy and his brother and sisters grew up as financially poor as people can be, but they were rich in all that mattered.

They had two parents who loved and wanted them, and although they were expected to work, they were not viewed as a means of income.

They were taught the value of family, religion, education, and hard work and were encouraged to leave the farm to provide a better life for future generations. With but a few exceptions, they did just that.

Their descendants include doctors, chemists, ranchers, executives, academics, and, of course, a cop.

Chapter 15

Compounding the Problem

All of the problems created by public entitlements existed when I was a child attending school in the 1980s. By the time I entered law enforcement in 1994, they had grown to unmanageable proportions.

It was during the late 1970s through the early 1990s that gangs began filtering out of Los Angeles, Chicago, and New York to infest cities large and small across the nation.

Crack was their foothold, and they set up shop in areas of cities and towns that had been all but abandoned by their governments. They moved into areas such as Section 8 neighborhoods and housing projects, which were already distressed and weakened by the degradation caused by entitlements and handouts.

United we stand, divided we fall.

Drug dealers battled each other for turf, and a wave of fear, crime, and hopelessness hung over the communities; the atmosphere was as heavy as the smell of gunpowder from the battle itself. Bodies littered the streets, and families were torn apart.

Black-on-black crime became a topic of well-disguised conversation in the media and across the nation. Many people became famous and wealthy by pointing blame at everything and everyone but the problem itself and the persons committing the crime.

Blacks who addressed the problem were called Uncle Toms by black activists, while whites were called racists. Even Bill Cosby, the father of all fathers, was ridiculed.

So many lives have been lost and so much money expended because we ignored the truth. Those brave enough to mention the large spike in crime within the "low-income" portion of the black community and its relationship with government handouts were quickly chastised and viciously attacked by the left for trying to take away from those "in need."

Although we may think they are, our politicians are not stupid, and they recognized the problem just as early as you and I did. It's just too much of a political hot potato, and no one wants to touch it. This is a long-term problem, and our politicians think in the short term—which is just until the next election.

God Bless America!

You must remember, one-third of our nation's population receives some form of government assistance, and whether Republican or Democrat, no one wants to lose that many votes.

Instead of addressing the actual problem, government did what it does best: write checks. It recognized that crime in the United States was at record levels, so federal grant money was used to hire more police officers, myself included—so I guess I should thank the government.

Corrections budgets were increased, and enough prison space was built to house the entire population of some countries. So began the greatest crackdown on crime in the history of the world. Stalin and Lenin would be jealous.

Citizens were becoming more vocal about intolerably high levels of crime and the negative effects it had on their lives. In response, community policing became a catch phrase in law enforcement, and departments were reorganized so that officers could work within smaller geographic areas. This would allow officers to tailor solutions at the neighborhood level.

Residents, fearful of crime, created neighborhood watches and held monthly meetings to share ideas and inform each other of occurrences. They looked to the police for solutions, and police agencies began to hone their problem-solving skills. Most police agencies adopted the Broken Windows Theory as the main thrust of their war on crime.

The basis behind this theory is simple and on the surface seems sound. Clean up neighborhoods, and residents will clean up their lives. Cities began to immediately dispatch work crews to address litter, graffiti, and overgrown yards and to pick up discarded household items left by roadsides.

Police departments began to work closely with housing code officers to address dilapidated structures, unhealthy living conditions, and abandoned vehicles. Owners of unsightly houses were forced to make repairs, with individual landlords expending thousands of dollars.

Government entitlement programs were utilized to build new or renovate existing homes in the heart of the ghetto. These houses were then sold to actual low-income persons at reduced prices, often less than the price of construction or renovation.

Police departments adopted a Zero Tolerance approach and began to target social crimes such as drinking in public, loitering, trespassing, and curfew violations. Suddenly people had "rap sheets" several pages thick and were indebted to the courts to the extent that their fines would never be paid off. Jails began to fill up.

God Bless America!

In essence, the ghetto received a new coat of paint. In reality, it was just a Band-Aid used to hide the wounds caused by the diseases of public entitlements and crack cocaine.

A few facts were never considered. These types of programs are very expensive and manpower intensive, and they require a long-term commitment. Even with the additional manpower provided by the COP's program, there just were not enough officers or money to bring about change on a large scale.

We failed to recognize that one of the primary factors in determining a person's behaviors are the social norms to which they are exposed. As soon as enforcement efforts were redirected to other areas, the crime and ghetto mentality resurfaced. The status quo resumed.

States and local communities can try to correct the problems with programs they devise. Their efforts, though, will always be smaller than the federal programs that created the problems in the first place. Here again, size does matter, and we are shaking the short stick.

People simply have too much time on their hands because they are not required to work.

United we stand, divided we fall.

Chapter 16

Entitlement Reform

We recognize the importance of history and teach it as part of the core curriculum in our schools. Why, then, do we ignore it as adults and disregard the wisdom espoused by those who came before us.

As early as the twelfth century, Chaucer noted that idle hands were the devil's workshop. It does not get any simpler than that. People with nothing to do will get into trouble.

Yet we hand out entitlements like candy at a Christmas parade, and then we get upset when people become dependent on them, are uneducated, or commit crime.

We must completely change the ways in which public entitlements are doled out. As mentioned, we need to be there to help people like Carl or those that have suffered catastrophic injuries. There is no way that they can take care of themselves, and we should extend a helping hand.

However, a bad knee, diabetes, a weak heart, or fear of public places would not automatically qualify one for a disability or other forms of entitlements. There are plenty of people who work every day with these types of injuries and illnesses.

Just the other day when I walked into Walmart, I was greeted by a woman who stood maybe two-and-a-half feet tall. Her limbs were contorted, which had to be uncomfortable, yet she still greeted me with a welcoming smile and a warm hello.

During that same visit, I was assisted with finding a product by a young man in a wheelchair. He informed me of its location and even rolled down the aisle to show me where it was.

We should give kudos to them for having that type of dedication and to Walmart for giving them the opportunity to display it.

In other words, people's disability would have to be so severe that they would be completely incapable of performing any type of work. Anything less would be denied.

There are jobs available for persons who will have been deemed to have non-qualifying ailments. However, accepting these jobs may require personal sacrifices such as relocating, working outside ones area of expertise, or perhaps even outside of ones preferences. But here again, these are sacrifices that many of us have had to make in our own lives.

Our nation simply cannot sustain the dependency on and abuse of the current system of entitlements. We must set a date, and after that date, any person requesting first-time assistance through an unearned government entitlement program would be subjected to a three-year lifetime cap. Once the three years are up, they are on their own unless they have a valid disability.

Persons receiving support through entitlement programs before that date would have a five-year limit imposed. The first year, they would be given full payment of any entitlement monies currently received. Each year for the next four years, their total payments would be reduced by 25 percent.

This would give them ample time to find a job and make other alterations to their lifestyle, which would ultimately lead to their becoming self-sufficient, independent, and productive members of society.

The process to qualify would also need to change and would require more than filling out a few forms on the Internet or a visit to the local human services office.

United we stand, divided we fall.

Currently, we make finding and qualifying for federal benefits far too easy. Just log onto the Internet and use the public benefits calculator to determine what you qualify for.

I completed the application, stating that I was a twenty-five-year-old, single mother of three with no income, and it returned 351 benefits for which I might qualify. Ridiculous!

Regular and random drug screening would be mandatory to receive any benefits. Regardless of what judges with lifetime appointments claim, this does not violate anyone's constitutional rights. They are voluntarily asking for assistance; it is not something that the government is forcing on them.

As a condition of employment, many of us have consented to supply a urine sample upon the request of our employer. This is not forced on us; we can chose not to accept the job if we do not wish to comply.

When people sign for their driver's license, they are giving their implied consent to submit to a blood, breath, or urine sample upon the request of a police officer if he suspects they are driving under the influence. Failure to take the tests is a criminal offense, which will result in the suspension of their license and possible jail time.

God Bless America!

If it is okay for purposes of employment or the privilege to drive, then it should be okay for someone wanting to live off of our tax dollars.

Because they are applying for government assistance, it's obvious that they cannot support themselves—which in turn means they cannot support any additions to their family. Birth control would be mandatory.

The birth control would have to be nonpermanent so that when the woman becomes independent, she would still have the ability to have children. It would also need to be injectable and administered by the state. We cannot trust her to take a pill each day, wear a patch, or implement some other form of birth control.

The injection would be administered when she reported for her mandatory drug screening, which would help reduce costs.

Studies show that some forms of injectable birth control are almost 100 percent effective in preventing pregnancy and typically cost $35-$70 per injection.

This is not sexist and aimed only at women. At present, the only forms of birth control for men are condoms or a vasectomy, and neither is a good choice.

United we stand, divided we fall.

Recipients would also be required to perform at least some work each week. Whether picking up roadside trash or volunteering at a local hospital, they must do something to earn our assistance. Looking for work or attending school would not count as employment-related activities. These are things that we have all done in addition to working.

There are thousands of temporary job placement agencies with plenty of jobs to be filled. This would be a good justification of preferential hiring practices, and if qualified, those on the public dole would get the job.

Recipients not agreeing to the terms would be denied all benefits; best of luck to them in their future endeavors. This would cause a southbound exodus to our borders because there would no longer be jobs available for illegal immigrants. Two birds, one stone.

God Bless America!

Chapter 17

Families and Children

Prior to addressing the problems associated with the abuse of public entitlements, we must first understand the problems associated with dysfunctional and criminally-minded families.

Most families would improve their standing and become self-supporting before the three-year cap would be met. However, something must be in place for the children of those who don't.

Every day, you hear about how we not only as a nation but as a world waste and abuse our natural resources and animal life. We argue about oil and offshore drilling and chain ourselves to trees to save owls. To the detriment of industry, we declare land off-limits because a previously unknown species of plant life has been discovered.

United we stand, divided we fall.

Billions of dollars are spent researching more eco-friendly fuels, studying global warming, or ironically, whether we may be entering a new ice age.

The same or greater level of importance should be placed on issues that immediately impact our society. Each of us should support charity and the preservation of all things, but priority must be given to America—particularly American children.

We need to look within and see the problems that exist today. Humanitarian organizations such as Doctors without Borders should be operating in cities throughout America, not Africa, Sri Lanka, Cambodia, or anywhere else.

They will get the same amount of pleasure and feel just as rewarded providing care to a child from the ghetto as they do from tending to a child in Uganda. The hugs of both are just as warm, and their eyes light up the same.

American churches should not be building and staffing orphanages in Vietnam when we so desperately need them here. Far too many of our own children need that type of love and care.

Just for a few years, those of us desiring to help others need to redirect our efforts and focus on Americans. This would be an excellent platform for our First Lady to champion!

God Bless America!

For most children, the direction that their lives will take begins the moment they are first brought home. Some will enter a loving and stable environment where they will be the apple of someone's eye. The parents will build their lives around the child, sacrificing to ensure that this young person will have all that she needs to grow into a productive and well-balanced member of society. She will be read bedtime stories and tucked in at night to fall asleep feeling safe and loved. He will be taken to the zoo, taught to swim, and taken to Boy Scouts. Such children will be disciplined for bad behavior and rewarded for good. Through their parents' example, they will see the importance of education, faith, and ambition and will be able to read and count before starting school.

Others, such as "Dum Dum," will be brought into a volatile and chaotic environment in which the only stability is provided by the streets. Typically, the home is headed by a single parent who views the child and his nine siblings as a means of income rather than as a precious gift.

The child will be exposed to the very worst that society has to offer and will witness his mother's promiscuous sex life, drug use, violence, abandonment, criminality, and overall inability to manage her own life, much less his.

United we stand, divided we fall.

His bed will be a pallet on the floor where he will fall asleep to the sounds of gunfire or of his mother being beaten by her newest baby's daddy. At times, he will awaken to the sounds of flash-bang grenades thrown by police officers as a search warrant is executed. Attempting to avoid arrest, the newest man in his life will stuff a bag of crack cocaine into his diaper. He will be taught to act out and to defy authority and will be rewarded for his bad behavior. Although he is yet too young to understand it, this will be defined as a learning disability and his mother will receive even more money. Seeking acceptance, he will join a gang, and this is where his real education will begin. He'll see and commit violence and will witness death—if not die himself.

Yet his fate and that of countless others could be avoided if we accept the need for change. The desire of the government is to keep families intact and to use foster care or other options only as a means of last resort. Some people, however, just do not need to be parents, and we must accept that.

Something outside of the government has to act as an external influence to provide for these children and get their lives back on track. The Department of Human Services has failed, and frankly, it was not the government's place to parent in the first place.

God Bless America!

Our cemeteries and prisons are filled with their failed attempts to intervene.

The June 8, 2011, edition of the *Arkansas Democrat Gazette* contained an article concerning a sixteen-year-old boy charged as an adult with capital murder stemming from an armed robbery.

The young man's attorney argued that the defendant would be better served in the juvenile justice system because "he was a fatherless boy, raised by a single mother in the gang-ridden and high-crime area of the city, who has been led astray by bad influences."

The prosecutor countered "there are plenty of people who grew up in bad environments...who grew to be strong and upstanding members of society."

The judge concluded that the young man had already served time in the juvenile system and had apparently learned nothing from it. The judge opted to have him stand trial as an adult.

All three are correct, and this one case disturbingly illustrates the failure of the child welfare system. It's obvious that the defense, prosecution, and judge were all referring to external influences and how they have or have not affected this person's life.   Whether a person grows up in the ghetto or in middle-class suburbia, he or she is a product of familial and environmental settings—good and bad. These factors determine our morals and values, the schools that we attend, the class of persons we associate with, and our religious affiliations, if any.

The young man mentioned in the article is the product of two failed human beings from a failed environment, which in turn produced a failure. You cannot breed two jackals in the wild and expect them to produce a lap dog.

However, with exposure to positive influence, most people have the ability to adapt their behavior to blend in with or rise above whatever setting they are in, be it familial, social, educational, or spiritual. Conversely, with exposure to negative influences, we also have the ability to fall below, and far too many are doing so.

In 2007, law enforcement arrested 2.18 million juveniles, 87,000 of which were placed in residential facilities. As with the adult population, black youth were arrested at much higher rates and accounted for 51 percent of all juvenile arrests for violent crimes. Most of these children came from failed families with long criminal histories.

Chapter 18

Inherited Pauperism and Criminality

The fact that crime runs in families has been known for many years and was first reported by Dr. Elisha Harris in 1874. A medical doctor by profession, Harris was also a well-respected sociologist—strongly interested in the conditions that led not only to ill-health but also to criminality and dependence on public charity.

Among his many accomplishments, Harris was a member of the New York Prison Association and served as its corresponding secretary. In this position, he recognized a recurrence of family names of persons incarcerated in county prisons—particularly in Ulster County.

United we stand, divided we fall.

Curious, he undertook a study to determine the cause of the recurrence. In the study, he was able to trace the family's lineage back six generations to a woman he referred to as "Margaret, Mother of Criminals."

Harris's study was first cited in an article written by Charles Brace, which appeared in the April 1875 edition of the *North American Review*. The article was written in response to the then ongoing debates concerning America's handling of the poor and the problems that the poor passed on to succeeding generations:

> An extraordinary instance of inherited pauperism was given recently at a meeting of the State Charities Aid Society, in New York, by Dr. E. Harris, registrar of the Board of Health.
>
> A pauper child, named Margaret, was suffered to grow up neglected in a village of Ulster County, New York, some eighty-five years since.
>
> She and two neglected sisters have begotten six generations of criminals and paupers. The total number of descendants now known, mainly of this pauper child Margaret, both living and dead, convicts, paupers, criminals, beggars, and vagrants, is six hundred and twenty-three.

God Bless America!

In a single generation there were seventeen children, of these only three died before maturity. Of the fourteen surviving, nine served an aggregate term of fifty years in the states' prisons for high crimes, and the other five were frequently in jails and almshouses. This mother of criminals cost the county hundreds of thousands of dollars.

Today, many researchers question the validity of the methods used by Harris due to the intentional omission of the more successful members of the family's lineage. The study has been cited as an example of the deliberate skewing of data by social scientists to advance the political agenda of the day.

However, public opinion, which is based largely on public perception, is the catalyst that forms our country's political agenda—social science only supports or refutes public opinion. The family (the Jukes) cited in Harris's research was but one example of inherited pauperism and its effect on criminality.

During the middle and latter portions of the nineteenth century, children were literally starving in the streets. Just as pauperism today—regardless of the cause—has led to increases in crime and the continuance of criminality from one generation to the next, so it did then. These factors helped form public opinion and set the political agenda—the nature of which is evident from the remainder of Brace's article.

Hoping to improve the plight of vagrant children Brace stated, *"It is of the first importance to the state that pauperism should not be inherited and transmitted, from the familiar scientific principle that inherited evils are intensified with each generation."*

He goes on to assert that the charity offered caused more harm than it did good and that pauper children should be removed from poorhouses and placed with "country families" at public expense.

Interestingly, the debates of 136 years ago are reminiscent of discussions taking place today concerning the detrimental effects of public entitlements.

> The English Poor Law, from which our own has been derived, fell into the mistake, even as far back as the reign of Elizabeth, of giving the English working classes the feeling that they had a right to relief on the part of the governing classes; or, in other words, that charity was a fund on which they could confidently depend…
>
> The poorest of the laboring classes lost the habit of self-support and the dignity of independence. The self-preserving instincts

were weakened; men and women showed no foresight, and knew that in their distress they could always depend on the state.... Relief was merely a right of the poor and a burden on the rich. It was given without sympathy or discrimination, and received without gratitude.

Neither class were benefited. Morality, too, became sapped along with self-respect. The pauper class were as dissolute as they were miserable, and, under the existing laws, found it for their advantage to perpetuate a breed of paupers. Families of beggars, prostitutes, and paupers, extending for three or four generations, were known to officials.

The product of the land, too, was consumed by these idle and miserable creatures, until in many places the poorest ate up all the profits of agriculture. Fields went to waste. Crime increased. Illegitimacy prevailed. The honest poor were degraded by the contact with the dependent and idle poor.

Discussions such as these led to many of the social reforms that began in the latter portion of the nineteenth century. Orphanages were opened, child labor laws were enacted, and the overall plight of vagrant or other needy children vastly improved.

United we stand, divided we fall.

This era of progress and reform ended with the creation of the modern welfare system, and once again we find that history repeats itself.

In 2001, an article titled "The concentration of offenders in families, and family criminality in the prediction of boys' delinquency" was published in the *Journal of Adolescence.*

Conducted in Pittsburg, the study involved 1395 boys aged 8, 11, and 14. The criminal backgrounds of three generations were examined in each boy's family and compared to each of the boy's juvenile records at the end of the three-year study.

The study found that criminality was highly concentrated in families and that 12 percent of families accounted for 59 percent of all arrested persons. On average, the most criminal 8 percent of families each contained five arrested persons.

Very few American studies have been conducted on inherited criminality, causing the authors to compare and validate their findings with those of other countries. Two primary reasons for the lack of data are the following:

- Difficulty in obtaining criminal records
- Difficulty in determining family lineage

In reference to the latter, the authors emphasized its complexity by stating, "In inner city settings, families are constantly changing and reconstituting, and it is difficult to determine who are the biological fathers, siblings, grandparents, and so forth." Despite the difficulties, the results are in line with those of studies conducted abroad.

A 1987 study in Birmingham, England, found that in families containing a convicted parent, 45 percent of the sons also had convictions. Additionally, a study conducted in Cambridge, England, found that 63 percent of boys with convicted fathers were themselves convicted versus only 30 percent of boys whose fathers had not been convicted.

The Pittsburgh study and numerous others suggest direct genetic predispositions to criminality. For example, identical twins have more similar rates of offending than do fraternal twins. Additionally, a 1993 study of adopted children conducted by Dr. Adrian Raine found that the offending of adopted children is significantly related to the offending of their biological parents rather than the offending of their adoptive parents.

Whether through genetics or environmental or other factors, pauperism and criminality are inheritable traits. For now, the causations are irrelevant— the problems are in place, and we must stop them from spreading to future generations. Once this issue is contained, the national focus can be redirected toward prevention.

United we stand, divided we fall.

Chapter 19

The Failure of the Foster Care System—A Plea for Faith-based Children's Homes

Today more than ever, poverty, dependence, welfare and crime are inextricably linked to single-parent families. Numerous studies have all come to the same conclusion—increases in welfare means increases in out-of-wedlock births.

In 1994, the Maryland National Association for the Advancement of Colored People concluded, "The ready access to a lifetime of welfare and free social service programs is a major contributory factor to the crime problems we face today."

United we stand, divided we fall.

This theory is supported by national research conducted by Hill and O'Neil, which showed that a 50 percent increase in welfare and food stamp benefits resulted in a 117 percent increase in crime rates among young black men.

Further in an article appearing in the *Atlantic Monthly* concerning the relationship between single-parent families and crime, the author stated, "The relationship is so strong that controlling for family configuration erases the relationship between race and crime and between low-income and crime."

Ignoring these facts, the official stance of the federal government is to keep families intact. With over one hundred federal programs benefiting children, the state of our most needy is deplorable, and the nation's return on investment is even worse.

Through a combination of direct outlays, tax credits, and exemptions, the federal government disperses more than $350 billion each year on child-related programs—a sum equivalent to $5,000 for each of the 75 million documented children living in America.

Despite or perhaps because of the vastness of the government's child-welfare system, many families still fail. When this happens to the point that rehabilitation is no longer an option, foster care is the preferred placement for the children. However, like the families the children come from, the foster care system is also a failure that is beyond rehabilitation.

Yearly, the foster care system serves over 780,000 children, with an average balance of 503,000 remaining in care. Of those exiting, just over half are reunited with their parents or guardians, 18 percent are adopted, and 8.5 percent are emancipated and leave the system without any family ties.

In May 2010, researchers from the Universities of Chicago and Washington released the results of the largest and most comprehensive study to have been conducted in the past two decades of young adults leaving foster care.

Known as the Midwest Study, the researchers found that 60 percent of young men who had been in foster care had been convicted of a crime, compared to only 10 percent of young men who had never been in the system. Women fared just as badly, with 75 percent receiving public assistance before age twenty-four. The researchers concluded,

> The picture that emerges from data we collected when they were 23 and 24 years old is disquieting, particularly if we measure their success in terms of self-sufficiency. Across a wide range of outcome measures, including postsecondary educational attainment,

United we stand, divided we fall.

employment, housing stability, public assistance receipt, and criminal justice system involvement, these former foster youth are faring poorly as a group both in an absolute sense and relative to young adults in the general population.

The individual causes of the failure of the child-welfare system are too numerous to elaborate on. Fault can only be consolidated and placed on the overall bureaucracy that beleaguers the system. However, one factor worthy of elaboration is the government's aversion of working with faith-based communities in the placement of children.

The care of orphans is a fundamental tenet of all faiths in America, and faith-based communities have a wealth of resources to offer. Their congregations are filled with people who are ready, willing, and able to serve as mentors, financial donors, and foster or adoptive parents.

Additionally, these organizations once provided sanctuary to many of our most needy through orphanages and children's homes. In contrast to the foster care system, these homes provided the children with structure, discipline, and stability. They were an environment in which the children could learn the values and life skills needed for self-betterment.

God Bless America!

With the liberalization and softening of America, these homes fell from acceptance. Child-welfare researchers and advocates deemed them to be cruel in that the children were required to work, pray, and behave. They feared the homes did not provide for the children's emotional, intellectual, and behavioral development.

However, research has proven these earlier fears to be false. On two separate occasions (1995 and 2002), Dr. Richard B. McKenzie conducted surveys of orphanage alumni who left residence prior to 1967.

Of the more than 2500 who responded, 90 percent stated they preferred their orphanage care over foster care, and 67 percent stated they would have chosen to stay at their orphanage rather than return to their homes. Over three-quarters of all the alumni listed their time spent in orphanage care as favorable while only 2 percent listed it as unfavorable. Of the respondents, 81 percent reported having never been abused while in the care of the orphanage, which also means that 19 percent of alumni reported one or more forms of abuse. Of those that reported being abused, 16 percent claimed physical, 9.7 percent mental, and 1.8 percent sexual. Dr. McKenzie noted that interpreting the results was difficult, as the forms of abuse were open to the definitions the individual respondents chose to apply. Also, different age groups could have viewed abuse differently. The report does not indicate any instances of serious abuse.

Although any abuse is abhorrent, the fact that it occurred should not rule out alternative forms of care. Were that to be a precluding factor, biological parents would also have to be ruled out—their rates of abuse are just as high. Childhelp.org estimates that in 2009, 6 million children were reported to the police as having been abused, and the general consensus among child advocates is that for every case reported, three aren't.

On a brighter note, as a group, the orphanage alumni far outpaced their age counterparts in the general population on a majority of social and economic measures.

- 8 percent higher rate of high school graduates
- 6.5 percent higher rate of college graduates
- Median income of $45,000
- Lower unemployment rate
- Significantly less usage of public assistance—6 percent.
- Only one had spent more than a year in jail and only 2.5 percent had spent any time in jail.
- A fault of note is that alumni reported a significantly higher rate of divorce.

God Bless America!

The study also found that the alumni were happier in their day-to-day adult lives than were members of the general population.

For fifty years, the National Opinion Research Center at the University of Chicago has assessed people's happiness through a one-question survey—"All things considered, how would you say things are going these days?" Respondents can choose between only three answers—"very happy," "somewhat happy," and "not too happy."

Dr. McKenzie asked this same question of the alumni respondents and compared the results to those of the general population.

	General Population	Orphanage Alumni
Very Happy	31.5%	58.3%
Somewhat Happy	55.6%	37.5%
Not Too Happy	12.0%	3.3%

The results of Dr. McKenzie's study of orphanage alumni stand in sharp contrast to those of former foster-care children. The type of care provided is the difference between success and failure, and we should want success for as many of our nation's children as possible.

The study not only refutes the conventional view that orphanages are not adequate for long-term

United we stand, divided we fall.

childcare; it supports my own personal experiences with one. I consider myself very fortunate to have been blessed with the best parents anyone could hope for, and I strive each day to be the man my father was and the human that my mother is.

I am so grateful for Palmer Home for Children in Columbus, Mississippi. It is where my mother was raised and the place that she still calls home to this day.

Since 1895 and with no federal assistance, Palmer has provided a home (not an institution) for scores of needy children. It is supported solely by the Presbyterian Church and private donations, which have been so great that they allow expansion into new cities.

If one denomination can accomplish something as great as Palmer, which in turn produces people as phenomenal as my mother, imagine how much better it would be if all denominations united to do the same. Excluding the founding of our great nation, the creation of faith-based children's homes on the scale needed today would be the single largest endeavor ever undertaken by private citizens and religious organizations in our nation's history.

It would require the unity of all churches and the creation of a nondenominational charitable organization focused on providing for children

God Bless America!

rather than promoting sectarian beliefs. The group that is most actively engaged with the children will undoubtedly win their hearts and ultimately their souls. Competition among the denominations is good, and the children will only benefit from it—but the in-fighting must be kept among the adults.

Currently, the various denominations maintain and staff numerous children's homes throughout the nation and often provide a very high quality of life—perhaps too high. Many offer on-site schooling, medical care, and abundant recreational activities, including horseback riding. While these are certainly nice, they limit availability and substantially increase the cost of care.

Most have transitioned from dormitory-style housing to cottages containing 8–10 children and two house parents. This provides the children with a more traditional family-style experience and is thought to facilitate interpersonal bonding. However, this type of housing is very expensive, with some reporting construction costs of $460,000 per cottage.

Although modern children's homes could serve as examples, the ultimate goal should be to replicate the "good quality" of care orphanages once provided. As Dr. McKenzie stated, "The world needs a Sam Walton of child-care—someone that can provide lots of kids with pretty good care at very good prices." Perhaps the solution is a melding of old and new—cottages for younger children during their formative years and dormitories for them during their teenage years.

This would provide them with all the benefits of the more traditional family experience while they are young and increasingly more independence as they age, preparing them for the transition into adulthood. This is not dissimilar from some of America's most elite boarding schools.

Although any needy child would benefit from this type of placement, not all will warrant it. Therefore, a smaller and more efficient version of the foster-care system would have to be maintained.

Jointly, these two services could efficiently serve not only neglected children but also the children of parents who have met the three-year cap on public entitlements and cannot muster the ability to provide for their own families.

For this to be effective, society would have to place the physical care of the children above matters of political correctness—racial preservation, transgender equality, sexual orientation, and so forth.

The National Association of Black Social Workers has long opposed the transracial adoption or rearing of black children, preferring instead to preserve

African ancestry. No matter how you look at it, this is racism in its purest form and is no different from the Aryan Nation pursuing the preservation of the white race.

That said, the celebration of one's ancestry is appropriate, but black heritage can be taught in other ways, not just from within black homes. Further, there are not enough black families to provide care for the number of black children needing it, and it is far better for them to grow up in a loving but predominately white environment than to be raised by the streets.

Also, the furtherance of homosexual rights should not be placed on the shoulders of these children. Although many homosexual couples could provide more-than-adequate homes, society just isn't ready for it.

This issue has already caused many faith-based agencies to cease providing adoption and foster services rather than sacrificing their religious convictions, and it could prevent them from participating in this type of program as well. Just as America is a faith-based nation, so, too, are these programs, and most faiths oppose the "act" of homosexuality—not the person, so don't take it personally.

This must be about the children—not our individual rights, individual beliefs, or individual desires.

United we stand, divided we fall.

Chapter 20

Funding Sources

With reductions in entitlement spending and the redirection of a portion of charitable giving, the goal of nationwide, residential child care could be realized with little if any additional costs to taxpayers, and may in fact result in significant savings.

Through attrition, the number of persons receiving public entitlements will shrink once the three-year cap is enacted—they will find jobs. Current and future welfare rolls will also be reduced once out-of-wedlock babies are no longer profitable.

Even if, collectively, these changes produced only marginal reductions in entitlement-based spending, the resulting savings would still be substantial. A mere 10 percent reduction would reap savings of $100 billion each year. These funds could then be redirected and applied to the direct care of needy children rather than being squandered by their parent(s).

United we stand, divided we fall.

With the three-year cap, families will no longer be entitled to a lifetime of free or subsidized housing, thereby reducing the overall number of housing units needed—development will cease. The $6 billion in annual tax credits currently provided to developers of these quasi-housing projects could then be extended to persons or corporations wishing to invest in the development of children's homes. Coupled with just 10 percent of the $100 billion in reductions and with proper incentives, this could offset large portions of, if not all, construction-related expenses.

Limiting land acquisition and construction costs to a national average of $50 million per development allows for 320 children's facilities to be built each year. This is equivalent to $50,000/child, with each facility being home to 1000 children. With a "Sam Walton of childcare," the costs could be significantly reduced, allowing for the construction of more homes each year.   The resulting economic benefits of such large-scale construction projects are incalculable and can only be compared to the jobs created from the construction of the interstate highway system. Everyone would benefit, and no new taxes would be required.

Additionally, Americans are the most generous people on the planet and, in 2009 alone, donated over $308 billion to charities—75 percent ($227 billion) of which came from individuals, not corporations. Any charitable giving is good, and people have the right to do as they please with their money. But imagine the possibilities if just for a few years we could redirect 20 percent ($60 billion) of our donations to the care of these children.

With all funds combined and allowing for administrative costs of 33 percent, $100 billion would be available for the direct care of our nation's most needy.

According to the Department of Agriculture (USDA), WIC provides nutritional services for 7 million infants and children each year. If each of these children were placed into church-based homes, the organization could provide over $14,285/year for the direct care of each child. This is significantly more than the $7,000–$9,000 the USDA estimates the average, middle-class American family ($57,000+) will spend per child in 2011.

All totaled, the National Poverty Center estimates that 16.4 million children live in poverty. When forced to do so, the parent(s) of most of these children will transition from government dependence to self-reliance, thereby reducing the number of children needing placement. If over time this resulted in a 30 percent reduction, the organization could provide $8,710 annually per child.

By transferring the care of these children from the ineptness of government to charitable hands, we could provide better care, create jobs, reduce waste and abuse, and prevent the economic collapse of America.

God Bless America!

Chapter 21

War on Drugs

The manufacture, distribution, and use of drugs is without a doubt the worst scourge to ever strike America. It affects all communities, families, and races equally and makes no distinction for socioeconomic standing.

I have seen doctors smoking weed, pharmacists popping Xanax, cops addicted to pain pills, moms hitting crack pipes, and lawyers shooting meth. Kids sell it in schools, gang members sell it on street corners, and doctors dispense it like candy.

It has been concealed in the bodies of dead soldiers, hidden in baby carriages, stuffed up butts or other orifices, stitched into the stomachs of animals, and strapped onto the backs of human mules during border crossings.

The most disgusting thing that I have ever seen happened with a young man who was well known to law enforcement. I observed him walking the railroad tracks after midnight on the day of his birthday. He was now about eighteen years and one hour old - a legal adult who was no longer under the jurisdiction of the juvenile court.

It is illegal for pedestrians to use railroad tracks, so I approached him to address the situation. When first making contact, I noticed a very strong odor of marijuana and that he was extremely nervous, which put me on alert. He had a history of carrying weapons.

In compliance with the Supreme Court's ruling, I conducted a Terry frisk and noticed several small bulges in his crotch area, which I thought, due to my training and experience, may be marijuana or some other illicit drug.

I read the young man his rights under Miranda, and he confessed that he had marijuana and crack concealed in his underwear. In a secure area, I asked him to unbuckle his pants so that we could retrieve the drugs.

As he did so, a horrible odor presented, which caused my partner and me to gag. Once he managed to peel his underwear away from his skin, I noticed that they were covered in green goo, as were the drugs and cash concealed within.

A string of the green goo hung from his penis, and it was obvious that he had a venereal disease.

God Bless America!

As I looked to my partner in disgust, he laughingly replied, "Dude, I'm glad you're the one who has to reach in there and not me."

I donned triple layers of protective gloving and dove right in. I recovered four bags of crack, six bags of marijuana, and approximately $1,500 cash.

Concerned as well as amused, I asked how long he had had this problem, and he replied that it had been a few weeks. Shocked, I informed him that he could receive free treatment at a health clinic and asked why he had not sought care. With no remorse, he stated, "I want to give this shit to all these crack-head bitches."

This should be a commercial for the Just Say No to Drugs campaign. If pus-covered packages of dope under someone's ball sac doesn't convince you to say no to drugs, nothing will—not even a war.

It is estimated that the federal government has spent over $1 trillion combating the war on drugs and that billions more have been spent at the local and state levels.

Despite all the time, money, and effort expended, more people use drugs on a regular basis today than ever before.

The *2010 National Survey on Drug Use and Health* estimated that 22.6 million Americans currently use

United we stand, divided we fall.

controlled substances, with marijuana being the most frequently cited.

According to the National Center for Victims of Crimes' website, more than half of the people arrested each year test positive for drugs and are "one of the leading causes of crime." Any cop will tell you that drugs are *the* leading cause of serious crime.

The Harrison Narcotics Tax Act of 1914 was the first law to restrict the distribution and use of certain drugs: opium and cocaine. Prior to this law, the sale and use of narcotics were unrestricted; a person could actually order cocaine from the Sears and Roebuck catalogue of the 1890s.

The War on Drugs began in 1970, with an official declaration by the Nixon administration in 1971. Although the figures are currently trending downward, we have averaged 20,000 homicides per year since the war's onset. In the prior decade, we averaged only 10,000 per year.

We have to either get serious about the War on Drugs or decriminalize drugs, because the policies and practices currently in place have failed.

A good model for reducing drug use, particularly marijuana, would be the government's approach to cigarette smoking.

God Bless America!

According to the CDC, 42 percent of Americans smoked cigarettes on a daily basis in 1965 versus only 20 percent in 2009. However, this reduction was not the result of criminalization and all-out police action against cigarettes. Instead media campaigns were launched to make us more aware of smoking's adverse health effects, which in turn transformed the smoker's status from socially acceptable to that of a leper. Businesses were held liable for the illegal sales of tobacco products and manufacturers were held liable for illnesses linked to their usage.

Most effectively, tobacco products were taxed beyond the comfort level of most people. Do the same for marijuana and apply the proceeds to rehabilitation—let the users pay for their own future care.

Chapter 22

Drug Law Reform

Only law-abiding citizens abide by the law. Laws do not stop criminals, they do not reduce crime, and, if not obeyed, they protect no one.

We have laws against murder, yet we have 20,000 murders per year. We have criminalized or restricted the right of law-abiding citizens to carry firearms, yet criminals are armed to the teeth. The same applies to our drug laws. They stop only those who would not have used them in the first place.

When drugs or alcohol are not available, addicts will sniff glue, huff paint, or suck Freon from a bottle. In prisons, the inmates brew their own form of alcohol known as Pruno. All that's needed are a fermentable substance (prunes or other fruit), sugar, a container, and time – which they have plenty of.

One morning while I was on my way to work, a call went out about a young girl who had apparently drowned in the bathtub. As I was just a few blocks

United we stand, divided we fall.

away, I went to assist the primary officer. By the time I got there, the paramedics had pulled her naked and lifeless body from the tub and were performing CPR.

A family member told us he thought she had "dusted off" while in the bathroom. Dusting off, also known as huffing, is when someone inhales dust remover from an aerosol can.

Gases inside the can are heavier than air, which forces the oxygen from the person's lungs. This shuts off the flow of oxygen to the brain and causes a blackout type of experience.

After "dusting off," she passed out, sank down in the tub, and drowned. Floating in the tub was an aerosol can that contained a spray intended for cleaning computer keyboards.

Such a shame—a beautiful, seventeen-year-old cheerleader so unhappy with life that she "dusts off" and dies alone in a bathtub.

Drug use is a mental-health issue and needs to be treated as such. Drug dealing is a crime, and although tough punishment is not the current trend, justice should be quick and severe.

We must stop making not only our drug laws, but all of our laws so complicated — period. In an effort to reduce prison overcrowding, Arkansas revamped many of its laws pertaining to narcotics and created

Act 570. This 164-page Act repealed or amended existing statutes, created new ones, and just made a convoluted mess of everything.

"Certified Drug-free Zones" were created, with enhanced penalties for persons selling drugs within 1000 feet of these locations. Zones include housing projects, skating rinks, parks, churches, and day care centers, among others.

The Act created or enhanced distinctions and penalties for selling different types of drugs based on drug type, schedule, and amount. Below is but one paragraph from this complex mess.

SECTION 50. Arkansas Code Title 5, Chapter 64, Subchapter 4 is amended to add a new section to read as follows:

5-64-427. Manufacture of a Schedule I or Schedule II controlled substance that is not methamphetamine or cocaine.

(a) This section does not apply to the manufacture of methamphetamine or cocaine, which is governed by § 5-64-423.

(b) Except as provided by this chapter, it is unlawful for a person to manufacture a Schedule I or Schedule II controlled substance.

(c) A person who violates this section upon conviction is guilty of a:

United we stand, divided we fall.

(1) Class C felony if the person manufactured by aggregate weight, including an adulterant or diluent less than two grams (2g) of a Schedule I or Schedule II controlled substance that is not methamphetamine or cocaine;

(2) Class B felony if the person manufactured by aggregate weight, including an adulterant or diluent:

(A) Two grams (2g) or more but less than twenty-eight grams (28g) of a Schedule I or Schedule II controlled substance that is not methamphetamine, cocaine, or a controlled substance listed in this subdivision (c)(2);

(B) Eighty (80) or more but less than one hundred sixty (160) dosage units of hydromorphone hydrochloride;

(C) Eighty (80) or more but less than one hundred sixty (160) dosage units of Lysergic Acid Diethylamide (LSD);

(D) One hundred sixty (160) dosage units or more regardless of weight for any other Schedule I or II depressant or hallucinogenic drug;

It should not be this complex. There is no reason for a person selling drugs in front of someone's home to get less time than someone doing the same at a housing project. Selling 2 grams of methamphetamine is no less destructive to society than selling 10 grams; you just have to sell it five times more often.

Prescribed drugs such as Hydrocodone and Xanax carry lesser penalties than methamphetamine or crack. These distinctions should not exist. Their medicinal value is negated once they're abused. The CDC claims that deaths from unintentional drug overdoses have more than doubled since 1999 and attributes the increase primarily to the abuse of prescription drugs.

It all boils down to the same thing: they are dope dealers. One is no worse than the other, and all should be sentenced equally. Later in this book, you will see my recommendations for prison reform and offender rehabilitation. If something similar to what I have suggested were implemented, the law could simply read as follows:

(1) Any person upon 1st conviction of illegally distributing a controlled substance shall be sentenced to 5 years in the State Penitentiary.

(a) After a minimum of 2 years of incarceration, and upon successful completion of the Offender Rehabilitation Program, he may be considered for parole.

Of course, laws must be a little more descriptive than the above example, but we must exercise restraint. As with the current tax code, complexity creates inequity.

However, the typical user deserves to go through some type of intensive rehabilitation process similar to the rehabilitation unit that I will discuss in a later chapter. Simple incarceration does users no good.

Many states have created drug courts to hear cases involving minor drug offenses, and most are experiencing certain levels of success. As part of the sentencing process, offenders must undergo drug counseling and limited rehabilitation. The court monitors their progress and has the authority to incarcerate those who do not meet the requirements or expectations.

Upon successful completion, the court can expunge the offense from the offender's criminal record, giving him or her a second chance at life. However, the offenders have to overcome many obstacles once they are released from the court's supervision, and remaining sober is difficult.

Some have the motivation within themselves to avoid returning to a life of drugs. Others do not, and the fear of going to prison should be so strong that it will serve as their inspiration to stay clean.

This will require prison reform. Prison must become something that is feared, dreaded, and to be avoided at all costs.

God Bless America!

Most states refer to their prison systems as the Department of Corrections. Nothing gets corrected there—nothing! It's more appropriate to refer to as the College of Criminal Behavior.

The criminal element of our society views prison as an institution of higher learning as well as a social networking club. They may not look forward to going there, but they know that once there, they will be able to hone their skills, learn the secrets to success from more experienced criminals, and develop contacts that will allow them to move up the criminal ladder. For many, it is a family reunion.

Criminality has existed since the dawn of time, and we are all prone to it due to the frailty of man. Our only deterrents are our morals and the fear of consequences.

Once God realized man was prone to sinful behavior, he did not threaten a simple slap on the wrist. He understood that punishment had to be so severe that when faced with temptation, man would obey all of His laws.

He created Hades and made it a nightmarish place where offenders would burn in lakes of fire and brimstone. He offered no parole—you would languish for all eternity in sorrow and torment.

Those of us of the Christian faith believe that once mankind realized how severe His retribution would be, He sent our Lord Jesus Christ to be a vessel for our forgiveness. His hopes were that we would reform and could avoid the fate that awaited us if we didn't.

However, we must ask for His forgiveness and then be willing to atone for our sins. In that light, our prisons should be viewed as hell on earth yet should offer an opportunity to achieve forgiveness once someone has atoned for his or her crimes.

God Bless America!

Chapter 23

Debunking Current Philosophy

Our jails and prisons are full of people who have never learned to function in normal society. Though extremely street-smart, they are socially illiterate, and most could no more function in polite society than a child raised by wolves.

The average inmate suffers from extreme addictions, is poorly educated, is prone to violence, and has little hope for self-improvement. They are our misfits, and the price to incarcerate them is $80 billion per year.

Due to the exorbitant costs of incarceration, many groups, particularly within conservative circles, are advocating reforms that include the following:

- Reductions in recidivism
- Increased use of parole and probation

United we stand, divided we fall.

- Geriatric release programs for prisoners age 50 and above
- Elimination of mandatory sentencing
- Privatization of prisons

Steps such as these will not work until substantial changes are made within the penal system. Most importantly, we must stop placing the rights of prisoners and criminals above those of law-abiding citizens.

Just the fact that recidivism rates are so high dispels the assumption that crime can be reduced through the increased use of probation or parole. Under current guidelines, both are ineffective, and half of all prisoners released in any given year are expected to return to prison within three years of their release.

Additionally, the vast majority of incarcerated persons have lengthy criminal histories and have been afforded the privilege of both services numerous times.

In a study spanning the three-year period from 1998–2000, the Metropolitan Police Department for Washington DC (MPDC) conducted local criminal histories on all persons arrested for homicide.

God Bless America!

The study found that of the 367 suspects arrested, only 15 **had not** been previously arrested by the MPDC for crimes of violence or property crimes such as burglary. The study found the following:

- 60 percent had between 1 and 5 prior arrests
- 25 percent had between 6 and 10 prior arrests
- 11 percent had 11 or more prior arrests

The average arrestee had 5.3 prior arrests with the MPDC, and one had 35.

Of all persons arrested, 83 percent had 1–5 prior arrests for crimes of violence; one had 12 priors. On average, each arrestee had 2.3 priors for violent crimes.

Not only did most have prior arrest records, the majority (70 percent) had prior convictions. More than 64 percent of all persons arrested for homicide had 1–5 prior convictions, and one had 32.

As for geriatric release programs, just because someone is older and more costly does not mean that he or she will no longer participate in crime.

Of the 13.6 million people arrested in 2009, 1.4 million were age 50 or above. Older persons can be just as prone to violence and thievery as younger.

United we stand, divided we fall.

Arrests of persons age 50 or above in 2009

Offense	Totals
Homicide	912
Rape	1,705
Robbery	3,199
Aggravated Assault	37,362
Weapons Violations	9,901
Drug Violations	99,170

No one, regardless of age, sex, creed, or race, deserves to be released from prison until he has served all of his time *or* proven that he is fit for reentry into society.

Incarceration is a costly and burdensome endeavor, and some feel that it could be better managed in the hands of private enterprise. Although doing so would allow for savings, only the government has the right to deprive a citizen of his freedom; thus, the punishment, care, and rehabilitation of offenders should remain a governmental function.

Savings can be realized within the current system if we can muster the strength and national unity required to effect the necessary changes.

God Bless America!

Chapter 24

Punishment

The incarceration of offenders became so burdensome and expensive only after the federal courts and government overextended their reaches. Both have allowed the prisoners too many rights and placed too many cumbersome regulations on the institutions.

They are prisoners; their lives should be miserable and their living conditions austere until they have earned something better.

Prisons are not all-inclusive resorts, and prisoners should not be afforded leisurely activities. They do not deserve televisions, libraries, or even visitations until they are actively on a path toward self-improvement.

Current prison conditions are not what our Founding Fathers had in mind in 1791 when they ratified the Eighth Amendment to our Constitution, protecting us from cruel and unusual punishment.

United we stand, divided we fall.

In fact, I think today they would question the judicial records of many that have been appointed to federal judgeships.

During the time of our Founding Fathers, punishments inflicted on criminals were more reminiscent of a modern horror film than of justifiable corrective actions.

Punishment was typically rendered the day of or shortly after a trial and consisted of intentional, prolonged suffering and humiliation. It would not have been unusual to see someone tarred and feathered and then restrained in the stocks for the crimes of fraud or speaking slanderous words.

Penalties for more severe crimes included whipping, stretching, disembowelment, public hanging, decapitation, or just plain torture.

During the Salem Witch Trials of the 1690s, an eighty-year-old man by the name of Giles Corey refused to enter a plea to allegations of being a witch. To induce a confession, the court ordered that peine forte et dure, a French legal term meaning strong and hard punishment, be inflicted. This is an archaic form of torture in which stones are piled onto the chest to restrict the ability to breath.

After surviving two days of excruciating torture, Corey died without offering a confession. This was life in Colonial America and was certainly still fresh in the minds of the Founding Fathers.

I doubt that even the most unreasonable and extreme among us would agree with that type of punishment; it's obviously cruel and unusual.

I do, however, think most would agree that a prisoner should not be automatically entitled to a television in his cell or to access to art materials, conjugal visits, or even the freedom to spend his days resting or engaging in leisurely activities. Access to anything other than a bed, food, and basic medical care should be earned and at their own expense.

We must completely revamp our prison system and recognize the distinction between punishment and rehabilitation. There are substantial differences.

Prisoners are not choir boys; they are incarcerated because of their animalistic and predatory behaviors. As such, they should enter a very bleak and austere environment in prison where they are provided only with the necessities to sustain natural life. It should not be a place in which they can become comfortable or even content with their surroundings.

General population should not exist; all prisoners should remain in their cells 23 hours a day. All meals should be taken there, and their only form of entertainment should be educational materials.

United we stand, divided we fall.

This would require fewer correctional officers and allow for a more orderly environment. It would reduce inmate crime and injuries, restore order, and effectively eliminate the criminal organizations operating behind prison walls.

Savings could also be realized through the elimination of specialized medical care provided to inmates. These costs have become financially burdensome to all states and are frequently cited by groups advocating the early release of elderly or ill inmates.

In 1976, the U.S. Supreme Court held that "deliberate indifference" to a prison inmate's health problems constituted cruel and unusual punishment and thus violated the Eighth Amendment to the Constitution.

As a result, inmates now have a constitutional right that no other American has: cost-free access to unlimited health care. The care provided is often better than that received by many law-abiding citizens and is now priced at over $6 billion per year.

In 2002, a controversy developed concerning a heart transplant given to a twice-convicted California inmate—serving a fourteen-year sentence for armed robbery.

Not only was this costly to California taxpayers—$1 million—but it also meant that for him to receive the heart, someone else had to die. Vital organs are a scarce commodity, and there were certainly one or more law-abiding citizens in need of that heart.

We should concern ourselves only with the natural life of an inmate. Those suffering from chronic or fatal illnesses should be made as comfortable as possible within the confines of prison and allowed to live out their natural lives.

United we stand, divided we fall.

Chapter 25

Rehabilitation

Once reforms have been implemented, and after a period of time in the prison environment, first- and second-time offenders would be offered the opportunity to move into the rehabilitation unit. This unit would be designed to teach the prisoner all the skills necessary to function in the free world.

This opportunity would be denied to the most egregious offenders: pedophiles, serial killers, and those sentenced to life terms.

The unit would be reflective of normal society, not the ghetto or current prisons. Its environment would allow for offenders to be molded into productive citizens rather than better criminals.

Prisoners would voluntarily enter the program and agree to a very structured life, one that affords them the opportunity for improvement. Just as we must do so in the free world, they would be required to work the number of hours required each week to achieve the standard of living they desire.

This would require self-sufficiency within the system and the ability to provide all that is needed for daily life, from growing one's own food to vehicle and building maintenance.

Inmate labor would be used for these positions, and inmates would be compensated based on the skill level and amount of work applied.

This not only allows them to learn a trade but also keeps them occupied and out of trouble. They would learn the value of work and how it can improve their lives through better housing and greater amenities—something most of them did not learn prior to incarceration.

For these prisoners, housing units could range from multiperson tents that are heated and cooled to single-man cells with many of the amenities offered in the free world. The more the prisoner works, the better he lives.

In recent years, several states have expanded their use of inmate labor and are reaping savings greater than expected. Inmates in Florida now grow their own vegetables, saving the state an estimated $2.4 million per year.

For even greater benefit to the states and inmates, we could apply the free market concept and create government-owned prison industries.

God Bless America!

These would be low-skilled, low-paying jobs that are not in competition with domestic production. Not only would this allow us to recapture jobs that have been lost to other countries, but profits derived from the industries would help offset the costs of incarceration.

Additionally, a portion of the inmates' earnings could be placed into savings accounts to be made available upon their release.

Education would also be a requirement to remain in the unit. Classes would consist of general education and literacy, character building, ethical behavior, and drug and alcohol rehabilitation. Life skills such as anger management, conflict resolution, communication, and parenting would be included in the curriculum.

If they had not graduated, they would be required to obtain a high school diploma or equivalent. Higher-learning courses would also be available just as they currently are; however, the prisoner would have to pay for them.

Should a prisoner act out, refuse to participate, or disrupt the rehabilitation process in any way, he would immediately be sent back to the prison system to finish out his sentence. There would be no slaps on the wrist.

After a period of time and upon successfully proving that they could reenter society as productive members, the prisoners would appear before the parole board. Their accomplishments while incarcerated would be weighed against the crimes they committed, and if warranted, they could receive a reduction in sentence and be released into a rigorous parole period.

This would require modifications to the current parole system, with parole officers having more interaction with parolees. The parole system would serve as a support system for the parolee and not just as a means of monitoring his progress.

Unfortunately, when people are released from prison, they are returned from whence they came. They have no job, no skills, and very little opportunity. Criminal records hover over them like black clouds, making them unattractive to potential employers.

Many do not have homes to return to, which is a requirement of parole. In desperation, they resort to halfway houses; many of which are nothing more than scams.

Typically, these are single-family houses or abandoned warehouses that have been subdivided into as many rooms as possible. I have seen houses holding up to twenty people, and warehouses up to one hundred.

God Bless America!

Locations such as these are merely business ventures for the owners, who couldn't care less about the welfare of the parolees.

The parolee is typically charged $100 per week in exchange for a bed and an address to give to his parole officer; this does not include any food or rehabilitation services. He also faces monetary fines for breaking house rules or not completing housework.

Parolees are also required to pay parole fees; in addition, they often have outstanding fines from previous convictions, suspended drivers licenses, and overdue child support. They are in the hole the day they move in and are destined for failure.

Several years ago, our narcotics unit began buying crack cocaine from within a "halfway house," which allowed us to obtain a search warrant and a closure order.

On the day of execution and as we burst through the door, we immediately observed a man engaged in sex with a known prostitute; a crack pipe, still hot from use, fell to the floor.

The two were immediately taken into custody, allowed to partially dress, and promptly removed from the home to be processed.

Our reports require that we obtain as much information on arrested persons as possible, including employment data. Typically, offenders state they are unemployed or receiving disability; therefore, I was a little shocked when he listed his title as director of the halfway house. No wonder recidivism rates are so high; the people in charge of parolees are high as well.

Our investigation revealed that the home was owned by a local attorney, who rented to a church that managed the "halfway house."

The "church" consisted of a man ordained a bishop by some fly-by-night organization. He'd never been formally trained in counseling, rehabilitation, or even the Bible; he'd only paid a processing fee.

There was no steeple, and his only worshippers were the parolees who paid to attend. I have a feeling that there will be a very special place in hell for him.

To address these types of problems, we can again turn to our legitimate churches and other charitable organizations as part of the solution. As with the homes for children, these organizations are the best option to guide parolees through their transition.

Once corrections are made within the system, anyone paroling from the rehabilitation unit would be required to spend a minimum of three months in an approved transitional home or facility. These would be staffed by professionals and monitored by the state, and they would provide a safe and structured environment for the parolees.

These facilities would consist of everything the parolees need to maximize their chances for success. They would assist with job placement and would offer twelve-step programs, weekly drug screening, and continuing education in life skills.

Even with unemployment nearing 10 percent, there are plenty of job opportunities available. Find a home being roofed, and you will find twenty illegal aliens, none of whom speak English.

It is estimated that 13 million illegal immigrants reside in the United States and that they make up a large portion of the low-skilled workforce. These are jobs that should be available to American workers, particularly the 800,000 persons on parole at any given time.

I would assume that a large portion of the current immigration problem would resolve itself if these jobs were made available to parolees and persons transitioning from our *reformed* welfare system.

Additionally, The Center for America estimates a current shortage of 2 million workers in the higher paying, blue-collar job market.

If reforms are made, persons exiting rehabilitation units will have received the training and experience necessary to fill these voids. Jobs such as these could provide them with enough financial stability to prevent them from returning to their former lives of crime.

Now for the hard part: forgiveness. Before the electronic age, a person could be released from prison, and no one was the wiser.

Today, people's criminal record follow them for the rest of their lives. It affects their employment and housing opportunities as well as their self-esteem. In many cases, it makes it all but impossible for them to successfully transition into society.

However, they merit clean slates upon successfully completing programs offering the same or greater degrees of rehabilitation and opportunity as have been described.

Their previous criminal histories should be available only to law enforcement. All fines should be forgiven, and they should be placed on reasonable child support repayment plans. Not only will this be necessary for successful reentry into society — they will have earned it!

There will, however, be people who will not reform regardless of the amount of help and opportunity with which they are provided. They simply do not belong in society.

No further opportunities would be extended to people returning to prison for a third, separate, and distinct conviction for a *non*-violent crime. They would serve out the entirety of their sentence in the austere and low-cost environment of the *reformed* prison system.

For those returning to prison for their third, separate, and distinct conviction for a violent crime — the sentence, would be death. There would be no appeals in that they are not being sentenced for any one crime, but for a series of three. Through the proposed reforms, they will have been twice provided with legitimate opportunities to rehabilitate. They will have been twice treated for their addictions, and will have been taught the skills needed to live a life free of crime. Society will have met its obligation to these types of offenders.

Such criminals have proven themselves unfit, and it does not matter if they are mentally unstable, slightly retarded, or just deranged. We do not need to spend $30,000–$100,000 a year to incarcerate them. They will have earned this sentence as well!

Chapter 26

Someone Better

Religion is just as much a cornerstone of a strong nation as it is of a strong individual, and it is frightening to think that it is not well founded in our government. We all need to believe that someone better than we are is in charge. This grounds us and provides us with a sense of purpose, belonging, and safety. It comforts us in times of fear, sorrow, or hardship and inspires us to move forward even when doing so makes no sense:

> Yea though I walk through the valley
> of the shadow of death, I will fear no evil:
> for Thou art with me; Thy rod and
> Thy staff they comfort me

Were it not for my faith, I would be too weak to pin my badge on each morning. My faith allows me to look past the horrors and see the person rather

United we stand, divided we fall.

than the blood, the anger, or the criminality. It allows me to see the child that the victim or perpetrator once was. It takes me back to when something as simple as a piece of candy could make him smile. A time when all he wanted to do was play with his friends, and their skin color did not matter. It helps me to see all that he could have been and all that we have lost.

Not only was our country founded in religion, but the very continent on which it resides was settled by persons seeking freedom *of* religion not freedom from it.

America is a melting pot of religious beliefs, races, and ethnicities, and our individual personalities are so different that it is difficult to believe we were able to unite and form the greatest nation the world has ever known.

Today it seems as though that unity may be slipping; we are becoming a disjointed nation. We have lost our purpose, focus, and patriotic zeal.

This was all stripped from us when we were ordered to remove God from our schools, our government, and, essentially, from public view. Yet He is as much a Founding Father of this nation as are George Washington, Thomas Jefferson, and John Hancock, and He should be celebrated as such. We

God Bless America!

have lost so much just so that a few would not be offended.

When I was a child and before we began our school day, we always rose and said a prayer, which was followed by the Pledge of Allegiance.

This was the most important lesson of the day because it taught us that before all else, we were O*ne Nation, under God, indivisible, with liberty and justice for all.*

United we stand, divided we fall.

.

Chapter 27

America Restored

Throughout the ages and in every society, there have always been people who fall into certain categories: rich or poor, lower and upper, the have's and have not's.

By and large, through our self-initiative, education, determination, and self-reliance, we create the opportunities that allow us to move up or down the social ladder.

Without some form of external influence, I will never associate with the likes of Bill Gates and Oprah Winfrey. This is not due to differences in morals or intelligence or because they are any better of a person than I am. It is simply that they created their own opportunities that propelled them into levels of society that I do not have the financial means to enter.

I do not begrudge those who have done better than I, nor do I expect there to be any type of

United we stand, divided we fall.

redistribution of wealth to bring me in line with them.

I am not wealthy and have had to skip meals so that my children could eat. I have worked 70+ hours per week most of my life to provide for my family and have never taken a penny in government assistance. However, I chose my status in life and am very proud of my place. I earned it!

Through public entitlements, the federal government has robbed an entire class of society of their pride. This has led to the destruction of families and to declines in literacy and education. It lowered our moral standards, created higher crime, and led to far too many deaths.

A new class has been added to the societal hierarchy of this country; we are now the working poor, the entitled, the middle class, and the upper class. The working poor have been overtaken by the entitled, and the distinction between the entitled and the middle class is rapidly becoming blurred.

It has to stop now! The government must admit the mistakes it has made and set itself and us on the road to success rather than failure. We must accept a few simple truths and build solutions around them.

We cannot sustain the drain on our society by those who are unwilling to support themselves.

God Bless America!

As you've seen, its impact is far greater than just economic.

Each of us takes some level of pride in the work that we perform. It grounds us and provides us with a sense of purpose. It motivates us to do better in all aspects of our lives so that we can attain the level of success that we desire. It's what keeps our dreams alive!

We must give all people the ability to dream. As long as financial crutches are available, people will use them. They will become dependent on them, and, ultimately, they will abuse them. They will lose all desire to dream of a better life because they lost their motivation.

We all must look past race. This is not a white problem or a black problem, it's an American problem. Whether black or white, no good citizen wants to live next door to a gang banger or drug dealer.

Ghettos do exist, and at the present time, they consist primarily of blacks who are dependent on the government. That's just the way that it is. It certainly does not mean that all blacks are dependent on the government or live in the ghetto; they aren't, and they don't.

Ghettos will diminish once we restore pride to the people living there. Once they have pride in their own accomplishments, we will see ghettos

United we stand, divided we fall.

transform into proud, working-class neighborhoods. That pride will be passed on to their children, who will have inherited the ability to dream of a better life for themselves.

Education is the foundation of a strong country, yet our educational system is in shambles. Rather than effectively addressing the special needs of children from the ghetto, we lowered the expectations of all of our students. Education begins at home, and if home is hell, that child will be behind. Common sense tells us that.

But once the parents of those children are in the workplace and their pride has been restored, they will spend more time at home.

Just like the rest of us, they will be tired, and home will be very inviting. Because they are at home, they may actually spend time reading or engaging in intelligent conversation with their children at the dinner table.

Now when that child enters school, he will be on a level playing field, and instead of acting out and being sent from the classroom of "smart kids," he may actually blurt out a correct answer. He will be proud of that and will realize that he knew the answer because he did his home-*work.*

We have to stop taking statistics at face value; numbers can be skewed to imply whatever you want them to. Unemployment is at 10 percent—yet drive through your town and count the number of "now hiring" signs that you see.

There are plenty of jobs out there and no excuse for someone not to have one. It wouldn't hurt them to flip burgers until something better comes along even if they were an executive earning six figures before losing their job.

As a people, we must demand that the government allow able-bodied persons to stand on their own two feet. Only the elderly or persons permanently incapable of providing for themselves should have access to entitlement programs for more than three years.

No matter what we do, some people will fail, and some families will fall apart. In some of those cases, children will be neglected and need care, so we have to have something in place to provide for them.

We must, however, remove the government from the job of raising children. We need to transition the responsibility from the Department of Human Services into the hands of caring, compassionate, and privately run organizations such as Palmer Home for Children.

Our private donations should be used to care for these children. They are our future, and we need to take an active interest in them. It's less expensive and much more effective to approach the situation in this way.

The majority of criminals from all races have their roots in the ghetto or ghetto mentality. Once people have their pride restored through their own self-reliance, hard work, and better education, the criminal population will naturally diminish.

We all make mistakes—though some are more severe than others. Offenders of all but the most egregious of offenses should be offered a legitimate chance to reform.

They need to be treated for their addictions and taught how to avoid them. They should be taught to work so that they can learn the skills that will allow them to dream of a better life, one not within prison walls. Once they have rehabilitated, they should be given a clean slate so that they can pursue their dreams.

The solutions that I have offered may not be the best and will certainly lead to challenges or complications that I have not thought of.

We have to start somewhere, though, and we can deal with problems as they arise. We can't just throw our hands up and surrender because the challenges are too great. It's not our nature!

We have to think creatively and with America's best interest in mind. It's time that we unite as a

God Bless America!

people and place our nation before our personal interests. There will be time to discuss those once our collective problems have been addressed.

The governance of this country must be restored into the hands of the people as was originally intended. Those whom we elect are but our representatives, not the supreme or final authorities.

United we stand, divided we fall.

Chapter 28

Political Reform

The problems discussed thus far can be attributed to many factors, but they all boil down to just one—a federal government that has exceeded its bounds.

Unfortunately, the federal government is what we often look to for change; however, we cannot depend on the source of the problem to also be the solution. Change must begin at the grassroots level, and we must take charge rather than simply talk about doing so.

We rant and rave about how corrupt the government is and how we distrust anyone who would consider a career in politics. We talk of excessive spending and political scandals, and each of us knows how to better govern the county.

The problem is that these are conversations held just among ourselves and only serve to increase our blood pressure. We are not afforded the opportunity

United we stand, divided we fall.

to discuss matters of importance with members of Congress nor are we asked to debate issues on Fox News.

The average person has no voice or platform from which to speak and be heard. Unlike Northup Grumman or General Electric, we cannot afford to pay $10,000 to attend congressional fund-raisers. The best that most of us can hope for are form letters from our Congressmen or other politicians asking for yet another contribution.

Because of this, the media and political analysts claim that Americans have become apathetic and do not care enough to get involved. Some even say that we have abdicated our right to self-rule—having surrendered that power to big business, political parties, and the elite within our society.

Although it was never intended that America be a pure democracy at the federal level, credence was to be given to the collective voice of the people through adequate representation. To this end, we have not only the privilege but also the duty to elect persons whom we think will best represent us and the nation in Congress. However, this duty is slowly being stripped from us; we do have a vote, but we do not get to choose whom we vote for. That is decided in backrooms, political party offices, and corporate boardrooms.

God Bless America!

The field of prospective candidates is greatly limited by the financial stranglehold that the two-party system has on elections. To raise the funds needed to effectively run for office, candidates must first obtain support and approval from the Republican or Democratic parties.

This creates party loyalists rather than American statesmen and rarely, except in recent times with the Tea Party movement, do third parties have a chance.

The debt crisis of 2011 proves beyond reasonable doubt just how dysfunctional and pathetic it has become. Our leaders have behaved like spoiled little children who did not get their way.

The in-fighting, partisanship, disagreement, and unbecoming conduct exhibited by some members of Congress, coupled with the lack of leadership exhibited by our President, have brought international shame on the country and placed her in financial peril.

Financial markets are in utter turmoil, and our credit rating has been downgraded for the first time in history. World leaders have lost confidence in our ability to not only meet our debts but even effectively govern ourselves.

China, of all places, has publicly stated, "Washington needs to cure its addiction to debt and learn to live within its means." We can't really be

United we stand, divided we fall.

mad at them, though; they hold a large amount of our debt and must be scared to death that we will declare bankruptcy.

Our financial problems are due not to a lack of revenue but rather to the Great Society programs that began in the mid-1960s.

Since the beginning of LBJ's War on Poverty, the United States has spent over $14 trillion dollars in aid to the so-called poor. It is no coincidence that our national debt totals this same amount.

But all is not lost; we can reverse the damage! We must turn our frustration into motivation and put this country back on track. It is time for everyday average Americans to take a stand.

Revolution is in the air, and hopefully, we can quell it with words and deeds before it turns to swords and guns.

God Bless America!

Chapter 29

Fair Elections

Albert Einstein once said, "You cannot solve a problem from the same consciousness that created it. You must learn to see the world anew."

It is time for us to reevaluate how our government is organized and how it operates. We must determine what works and what doesn't and then have the fortitude to demand that the necessary changes be made.

First among the reforms should be the methods used to elect our officials. The primary election system in use by most states pits the two dominate political parties, rather than the most qualified candidates, against each other. This often compels voters to tow party lines rather than follow their hearts and instinct.

Arkansas's 2006 race for the Office of Attorney General is a glaring illustration of this point. The most qualified and popular candidates all came

United we stand, divided we fall.

from the Democratic ticket, and the primary election ended without a clear victor. Dustin McDaniel received 38 percent of the votes, Paul Suskie 32 percent, and Robert Herzfeld 29 percent. This resulted in a very difficult runoff between McDaniel and Suskie.

Suskie was a very conservative Democrat and often referred to as a closet Republican, whereas McDaniel was considered to be slightly more progressive.

Both candidates appealed strongly to law enforcement—McDaniel from his service as a police officer and Suskie from his strong prosecutorial stance against drug dealers and nuisance properties.

During the runoff, the progressive portion of the Democratic Party sided with McDaniel and the more conservative with Suskie. The run-off ended with McDaniel receiving 50.8 percent of the votes and Suskie 49.2 percent. Less than 3,000 votes separated the two.

Paul is a close friend of mine, and during the campaign and post-election, I found that he appealed strongly to Republican voters. Many with whom I spoke regretted not having had the opportunity to cast their vote for him.

Arkansas is an open primary, meaning voters can choose at the polls to vote on the Democratic or Republican tickets but cannot vote for candidates from both.

The race for attorney general was one of only a few that had Democratic candidates with Republican appeal, which was not enough incentive to cause a Republican to cross over and vote in the Democratic primary.

As a result, Paul lost potentially thousands of votes from Republicans who would have cast their votes for him had they been afforded the opportunity.

Had this not been the case, I feel that Paul would have won the primary with a clear margin to face the Republican candidate in the general election.

This leads us to another conundrum. In this particular election, the two most qualified and popular candidates were both Democrats, only one of whom could advance to the general election to face the winner of the Republican primary. In the end, each of the two parties must be represented in general elections.

Some states, however, have adopted a Top Two system for their primary elections. This system consists of an open primary in which voters can choose between all of the candidates regardless of party affiliation.

As candidates are representing themselves rather than a political party, they are not required to list party affiliation, if any, on the ballot. The two candidates receiving the most votes move on to the general election, even if they are from the same party. This allows voters in general elections to choose between the two candidates that the majority of other voters from their state deemed most qualified rather than just between a Republican and a Democrat.

As one might imagine, the largest and most powerful opponents of the Top Two system for primary elections are the Republican and Democrat parties. Using this system in all states would eliminate the monopoly these two parties currently have in most elections, and they would no longer be guaranteed representation in general elections. Although this would not render them powerless, it would certainly reduce their influence.

These types of changes must be made by the individual states through either initiatives or legislative propositions; the method used may vary by state.

All states allow legislative propositions to be placed on the ballot by members of the state's legislative body.

For this to be initiated by citizens requires that enough people contact members of their state's legislature to entice them to propose it. This is the most common method and the most likely to be approved.

Currently, only twenty-four states allow direct actions by citizens through initiatives. In these states, citizens can have measures placed on the ballot by petition upon obtaining a minimum number of signatures.

This gives *us* the opportunity to be a part of the legislative process in that *we* can start movements to obtain support for *our* propositions.

If enough support is garnered, it will be placed on the ballot and put before the voters to decide. This is more representative of government by the people and is something that citizens of all states should lobby for.

To find out more about the process and which measures the various states allow, you can visit the Initiative and Referendum Institute at **www.iandrinstitute.org**.

United we stand, divided we fall.

Chapter 30

Campaign Finance Reform

Currently, candidates and elected officials are far too dependent on large donations from wealthy individuals, corporations, political parties, political action committees, and other special interests groups. This, in turn, makes candidates nothing more than indentured servants to high dollar contributors rather than representatives of the people.

Campaign Finance Reform has been on the table for a number of years, and several states have enacted legislation that greatly restricts the influence special interests and other groups have in campaigns.

New York City implemented landmark reforms in 1988 through the enactment of the Multiple Match Public Financing System. It has been hugely successful and is often cited as a model for state-by-state reform.

United we stand, divided we fall.

Arizona and other states have also enacted legislation similar to that of New York City; however, some aspects have faced legal challenges. Both systems allow public funds to be used to finance political campaigns, and the U.S. Supreme Court found portions of Arizona's system to be unconstitutional.

In its June 27, 2011, ruling, the Court found that Arizona's Clean Elections Fund created an "air of equality"—not inequality—thereby depriving privately financed candidates of their right to free speech. The law tied the amount of public financing (average Joe) to the spending of privately financed (political party) candidates.

In other words, the more the privately financed candidate spent, the more the others received in public financing. The Court felt that this created too much of a level playing field.

However, the Court did not call into question the "wisdom of public financing as a means of funding political candidacy." In fact, it implicitly stated it was not their "business." Therefore, a method needs to be developed that does not include the financial triggers that were a part of Arizona's system.

The Fair Elections Now Act is also a strong contender in the fight for reforms. It has drawn strong bipartisan support from over two hundred members of Congress and seems to be gaining momentum.

However, this Act relies solely on public subsidies and places too much of a burden on taxpayers. Therefore, a hybrid of the systems in use by New York City and the state of Arizona stands as a viable solution.

The New York City model consists of four elements:

- Small donor multiple matches
- A qualifying threshold for candidacy
- Voluntary spending limits
- Enhanced disclosure requirements

Multiple Small Donor Matches

Matching funds are not a new concept. Since 1976, the Federal Elections Campaign Act has provided matching funds at a 1-to-1 ratio for the first $250 of each contribution to participating candidates in presidential primary elections.

The New York City model, however, matches the first $175 of eligible donations at a rate of 6-to-1. The distinction is that only donations from individuals within the city are eligible to be matched. Candidates are barred from accepting contributions from corporations, LLCs, LLPs, and partnerships.

This encourages candidates to seek smaller donations from actual constituents rather than pandering to special-interest groups for larger donations.

Qualifying Criteria

Before becoming eligible for matching funds, candidates must receive enough donations from constituents to meet the qualifying threshold. The threshold increases in proportion to the level of office sought.

Mayoral candidates must raise a minimum of $250,000 from no less than one thousand qualified voters, whereas someone running for city council would need to raise only $5000 from seventy-five actual constituents.

Only the first $175 dollars of any one contribution from an individual constituent counts toward the qualifying threshold. Contributions from other sources are not counted, which results in candidates having to rely on constituent support from the very beginning.

Voluntary Spending Limits

Along with other limitations, candidates must agree to expenditure limits before they can receive matching funds. The amount received in matching funds cannot exceed 55 percent of their expenditure limit, which maintains the value of constituent contributions.

In 2009, mayoral candidates could spend a maximum of $6.1 million, including up to $3.3 million in matching funds. Candidates for city council were limited to $161,000 with matching funds of up to $55,550.

Enhanced Disclosure

Not only does this system encourage candidates to develop and maintain contact with actual voters, it in fact mandates it. Should candidates not do so from the very beginning, they will not make it onto the ballot.

This system empowers voters, giving them knowledge and access via mandatory disclosure, mandatory public debates, and easy-to-understand voter guides. Even nonparticipating candidates must adhere to the disclosure requirements.

The 2009 election cycle contained sixteen mandatory reporting dates, and as the election date neared, candidates were required to report on a daily basis. This allowed voters to stay abreast with how much money candidates were receiving and from whom it was received: true transparency.

United we stand, divided we fall.

The disclosures are maintained by the Campaign Finance Board, an independent and non-partisan city agency tasked with the oversight and management of city elections. The disclosures are posted into a searchable database on the agency's website.

The city also prints voter guides and mails a copy to every household in the city that contains a registered voter. The guides include the following:

- the candidate's photograph
- party affiliation
- offices held
- current and prior occupations
- educational background

The guides also contain brief statements from the candidates conveying their principles, platforms, and views.

Although the system is voluntary, it has achieved outstanding levels of candidate participation. In 2009, 76 percent of all candidates financed their primary campaigns using this program.

With slight modifications and if adopted by the states, a system such as that of New York City could be applied to campaigns for all offices up to and including congressional candidates.

Just imagine how much better the country would be if 76 percent of Congress felt more indebted to

God Bless America!

individual voters than to special interest groups or political parties.

The downfall is that this system is dependent on public funds. However, the method used by Arizona makes use of monies raised through civil penalties, criminal fines, and voluntary $5 donations from state income tax returns.

Since its enactment, Arizona's Citizens Clean Elections Fund has raised $145 million and has financed over 1100 candidates.

The citizens of Arizona are so pleased with the CCEF that they voluntarily contribute 47 percent of all funds needed to finance the system. Court assessments on civil penalties and criminal fines pay the remaining 53 percent.

As previously mentioned, the Supreme Court declared only the payment-to-candidates portion of Arizona's system unconstitutional, not the method through which it was financed.

Therefore, a viable solution would be for each state to adapt NYC's multiple match system for the disbursement of funds and to finance it using the following:

- voluntary $5 individual contributions
- 10 percent levy on court fines and penalties

Eligible candidates would receive a lump sum payment equal to 50 percent of the amount spent

by the last winning candidate for the office being
sought. They would also receive matching funds at
a 6-1 rate for the first $200 of contributions from
individuals.

As with the NYC model, contributions from corporations, LLCs, LLPs, and partnerships would be
prohibited.

Estimated costs for the 2008 congressional campaigns have been placed at $1.6 billion. On average,
candidates spent $1.1 million vying for a seat in the
House and $6.5 million for a seat in the Senate.

To offset the costs of congressional campaigns, a
10 percent surcharge could be added to the penalties and fines imposed by the federal courts, which
totaled $6.7 billion in 2010. In the case of 2011, this
would have generated an additional $670 million
for the fund—42 percent of total costs. Funds would
be distributed to the states based on their number of
congressional seats or other criteria.

Few Americans currently choose to participate in
the FECA to fund presidential campaigns. The reason is simple: we do not feel that it makes one bit of
difference, so why waste a dollar.

If, however, a system similar to Clean Elections
were instituted, most federal taxpayers would certainly contribute an additional $5 to a fund that
helps pay for congressional campaigns. This alone

would generate $500 million; combined with federal surcharges on fines and penalties, it would total $1.1 billion.

Seventy percent of the total needed to fund congressional campaigns could be raised with no more costs to taxpayers than a $5 contribution.

If necessary, the remaining balance could be raised by placing a 5 percent surcharge on contributions received by candidates from sources other than individuals.

To be compliant with the Supreme Court's ruling, entry into the funding system must be voluntary and will require action by the people to encourage candidates to participate.

We would have to make it clearly known that the vote of everyday Americans would be cast only for participating candidates.

*Other than my personal opinions, most of the information for this chapter was compiled from the Brennan Institute of Justice's report: **Small Donor Matching Funds: The NYC Election Experience** and information provided by the New York City Campaign Finance Board.*

United we stand, divided we fall.

Chapter 31

Twenty-first–Century Government

Unless you are employed within the political circus arena, it is all but impossible to stay abreast of governmental affairs. This is particularly true with Congress, where thousands of bills are proposed each year.

Some, such as the renaming of national parks or buildings, are of no concern to most Americans and have little meaning to anyone other than the sponsors.

Others, however, are more important and directly affect our wallets, our values, and our way of life. Bills such as these should be subject to full disclosure in a clear and concise manner and should be open to public debate.

United we stand, divided we fall.

That's how our government was intended to operate when founded; we just outgrew it. The original thirteen states consisted of less than 3 million residents, and all but the most rural kept abreast of current events.

Government was localized, and most matters were decided at the county or state levels. Town squares, churches, and taverns were the social networking sites of the day. They were places where representatives of government would interact with their constituency and seek their input on legislation as well as their guidance on the governance of the city, county, state, or nation.

Today, town squares are but nostalgic reflections of our past, and the hectic pace of life, combined with the broadness and complexities of government, makes it difficult, if not impossible, for citizens to stay informed. Doing so just at the most basic level—local government—would require attending several meetings each month.

However, technology is available that would allow for the creation of a more open, transparent, and participatory virtual government. All that is needed is currently in place or readily accessible; we simply have not availed ourselves of its use.

Envision a social networking website similar to Facebook or MySpace designed to facilitate the flow of information and communication between the government and the citizenry.

One centralized location could allow verified constituents direct access to their elected officials from all levels of government—city, county, state, and federal. To avoid confusion and reduce clutter, each level would have a unique section within the site. The user would simply select the section he or she wished to view.

From here, users could access all pending and proposed legislation currently before their elected officials along with the officials' opinion of the legislation and the stance that they intend to take.

Through online polling, verified constituents would be allowed to cast their vote for or against the matter to be decided. This would serve two purposes.

First, elected officials could use the results to determine how to best represent their constituents. Second, the results of the polls, along with how the officials voted, would be posted, allowing constituents to see whether the majority had been truly represented.

To recreate the town square of yesteryear, officials could host regularly scheduled video conferences to discuss the issues, give updates, and seek input. Additionally, online debates between officials with differing opinions could be held, giving voters the opportunity to see both sides of the issue and the ability to ask questions in real time.

The possibilities are endless; we are limited only by our imaginations and—more importantly—our willingness to participate.

These types of reforms would allow the American Vision as best expressed by President Abraham Lincoln to once again be realized: government of the people, by the people, and for the people.

Conclusion

Although it actually took only a short time to write this book, it has been at least seventeen years in the making. The opinions and solutions that I have offered stem from my exposure to parts of the United States that most people, fortunately, never have to see.

I have spent most of my career attempting to improve my local community through some very creative programs. In the mid-1990s, I became an instructor in Smart Choices, Better Chances, a program sponsored by my state's attorney general's office. Its purpose was to send police officers into elementary schools to teach children that there are consequences for all actions taken, whether good or bad.

In the late 1990s, I became involved with our local police athletic league. This is a fantastic program aimed at children from low-income neighborhoods; police officers and local citizens coach kids in athletic programs such as football, baseball, golf, and archery.

This was probably one of the most rewarding experiences I have ever had in that the kids were so grateful that an adult was taking an interest in them. Unfortunately, rarely did a parent attend.

It was through this program that I met Paul Suskie, who at the time was one of our assistant city attorneys. We both had an earnest desire to improve our community, and it was only natural that we developed a friendship.

We enjoyed working with the children and often discussed ways that we, as public servants, could make their lives permanently better.

Over lunch one afternoon, we were discussing various programs for children and whether we would be interested in implementing them. He mentioned Smart Choices, Better Chances, and I told him that I had already been through the class.

I warned him that the instructor was very good-looking, which made it difficult for police officers to pay attention. He asked me to describe her, and when I was done, he said, "Dude, that's my wife."

Even with that, our friendship only grew stronger, and together we devised the S.A.F.E. Team, a program that unites all of a city's resources to fight crime.

Rather than relying solely on the powers of arrest and with the goal of revitalizing neighborhoods, we evicted criminal tenants and closed problematic properties.

We obtained unparalleled success and effected great changes in our community. With this program, we were actually able to restore life to some of our worst neighborhoods.

Paul moved on to higher appointed positions within state government and is now employed in the private sector. With his absence, the team fell apart, and all of our accomplishments have now been reversed.

Paul served as an example in many parts of this book—most notably, my description of who politicians are and what they should stand for.

He comes from what most would consider a privileged background and was certainly never exposed to any of the bad the world had to offer. However, for the S.A.F.E Team to be effective, he needed to see it firsthand. Therefore, we spent many weeks and months inside the ghetto, and he gained a new perspective of the world.

Paul has been groomed since early childhood for a life in politics and served as president of Boys State and his college fraternity. His everyday family photos look like political advertisements or an ad for the all-American family. They are simply good people.

Paul is a Democrat and I'm a Centrist, but we are equally American—with undying love for God

United we stand, divided we fall.

and Country. Often this leads to very interesting and heated political debates and sometimes ends with us chest to chest. We are both very resolute.

Most importantly, though, with every subject we discussed, Paul would always ask, "Are we doing this because it's right?" followed by, "If so, let's simply do it."

What more can you ask of a person than that he be a decisive leader willing to place doing what is right before all else? We deserve no less, and I hope that all politicians will adopt this attitude as their own.

Despite all of the programs that Paul and I participated in and the successes that we achieved, things have only gotten worse. The efforts that we made were always overshadowed by the magnitude of the federal programs that created the problems in the first place.

Like many other officers, I finally realized that the issues we face today cannot be changed by law enforcement or local government. They are societal problems that can be changed only at the highest levels of our government.

Angst, fear, and regret, along with disappointment and the feeling of failure, were my inspiration for this book, and nothing here is intended to be insulting or hurtful to anyone. I hope that I have

God Bless America!

offered you a view of the world that we have created, albeit from a safe distance.

I did not write this book alone; the souls of the many dead to whom I have been exposed were my companions. I hope that I have portrayed their stories well and given you a better understanding of what led to their deaths and how we can prevent more from occurring. I know that they, too, must now believe the cycle must end. God bless them all, and may they finally find their peace. I need some rest!

Wake Up America!

United we stand, divided we fall.